MW01536122

RAISED BED GARDENING AND COMPANION PLANTING FOR BEGINNERS

The Ultimate Guide to Growing Organic Vegetables and Plants. Tips & Tricks to Help Gardeners Cultivate a Rewarding Garden

GREEN THUMB COLLECTION
GARDENING IDEAS

TABLE OF CONTENTS

PART I

RAISED BED GARDENING

FOR BEGINNERS

INTRODUCTION

You may well be wondering why on earth a raised bed garden is any easier than planting vegetables straight into the soil. Or why indeed I have titled this as I have done, by insinuating that raised bed gardening is easy.

Well, the fact is that in my opinion, growing vegetables in a raised bed is by far the easiest way of growing great vegetables without the huge labor involved when growing the traditional way.

However, I must clarify that by saying raised bed gardening has been around since the beginning of time, and although it has received more prominence as of late, it is by no means a new concept – think of the hanging gardens of Babylon!

In this publication, I intend to spell out, in layman's terms, just what it means to grow vegetables (or fruit, flowers etc) in a raised bed. How to construct a raised bed, simply and easily, including the different materials that can be used at minimal cost wherever possible, even how to convert your raised bed into a temporary greenhouse, at minimum cost in easy-to-follow steps.

The raised bed gardener can spend longer tending to his plants than the average vegetable gardener, simply because he (or she) is not spending their valuable time digging over the soil and clearing out weeds. For this reason only the raised bed is preferable for those who are working all day and have limited time to spend in the evening tending their vegetable plot.

Advantages of a raised bed garden

There are several advantages that a raised bed has over planting straight into the ground, some of these are as follows:

With a raised bed, it does not matter what quality your garden soil is, or indeed what the drainage is like, as this is all added when forming your raised bed garden.

Easy to service/maintain

With a raised bed you have the advantage of height, which means that you do not have to bend over as far to take care of your vegetables. This is particularly advantageous if you are prone to suffer from back-ache.

Weed-free

A raised bed is not troubled to nearly the same extent by the incursion of weeds, as all the soil/compost mix is freshly added. For any weeds that do appear, they are easier to remove as the compost mix does not compact like garden soil.

It is far easier to control destructive pests within a raised bed garden. This is simply because you are off the ground, and so keeping a natural barrier up in front of creeping pests like garden slugs.

With a slightly higher raised bed of around two feet, then you are not troubled quite as much with carrot fly for instance, who tend to be low fliers.

So out with back-breaking weeding tasks, along with digging over waterlogged soil and filtering out rocks and stones, in with easy gardening methods for the busy householder, and fresh vegetables for the whole family with the minimum of hassle.

The Benefits

More so, raised garden beds prove to be important when it comes to protecting plants from certain pests, such as snails or slugs, for example, and in making sure that plants get equal amounts of water and humidity. This is because soil that's placed in a closed spot is warmer than soil that's just on the ground.

Meanwhile, the bottoms of raised garden beds are open—which means that water could easily be absorbed by the roots, as opposed to being absorbed by the stems, which would do nothing good for the plants. This way, the plants would get the nutrients that they need—without any blockage!

This book is therefore aimed to provide you with all the essential knowledge and tips you will require to grow healthy and nutritious vegetables at home with minimal effort and investment.

This book contains various steps and strategies on how to make sure that you're able to create a great raised bed garden! With this book, you'll learn exactly why you need this type of garden, the tools that you need to make it, tips on how to maintain the garden—and more!

Start reading this book now and be a master of raised bed gardening in no time! Thanks again for downloading this book, I hope you enjoy it!

CHAPTER 1. WHY THE RAISED BED SYSTEM

Having started to use raised beds, I will confess to having scratched my head and wondered why I didn't do it sooner. I'd always worked with bare soil, thinking raised beds would take up too much space and I've done well. Since I moved to raised beds, partly for neatness, partly to stop accidental damage, and partly to help with crop rotation and managing what is planted where, I have found that my productivity is up, my weeding and digging is down, and my vegetable plot is far more productive and easier to manage than ever before!

My first move to raised beds came when I moved to an overgrown allotment that was shoulder deep in weeds. I'd seen people build raised beds before, spending large sums of money on converting their plot and I had wondered why they did it. I know two gardeners that built raised beds to make their vegetable plot accessible for a disabled child, which is an excellent solution.

However, I inherited this plot that was covered in weeds, and as I was clearing them, I tripped over something and discovered a wooden plank. Further clearing revealed several raised beds. I left them in place and started to work them as it was too difficult to remove them and the bark paths.

As I started working with the raised beds, I started to realize just how many benefits they had. It was much easier to condition the soil, easier to get between the beds and I didn't get as covered in mud, which meant a happy marriage as I didn't traipse dirt into the house and car. After dismissing raised beds for such a long time, I was surprised by how much easier they made vegetable gardening. When everyone was busy digging their soil over as summer ended, I covered the beds with manure and black plastic and left them until spring, knowing I had less work to do. Spring came, and everyone else was digging all the winter weeds out of their beds while I uncovered the beds and started planting.

Raised beds are great if you are growing in an area with poor soil. One part of my vegetable plot was about three inches of soil on top of hard-core rubble which isn't ideal for planting anything in. With a raised bed on it, I've added about eight inches of soil, so there is plenty of soil for me to grow many types of vegetables, except root vegetables. It has turned an unproductive area of my allotment into a very productive vegetable garden. Of course, if you have good soil under your raised bed you can easily plant crops that need deeper roots, e.g. potatoes (personally I grow them in bags so that I don't find potato plants growing all over my plot).

If your soil is poor, lacking in nutrients or has any problems, then a raised bed is ideal because instead of amending all the soil in your vegetable garden you can amend the soil within the raised bed and leave the rest alone. Amending the soil for the whole plot can be very time consuming and quite expensive, yet with a raised bed you can just amend a small area at a time, making it more manageable.

One of my vegetable plots has heavy clay soil, which is difficult to grow many vegetables in. Digging the entire area over was very hard work, and so I dug in manure and some horticultural sand which over two or three years loosened up the soil. Had I used raised beds this would have been a much easier process because I would have just added the correct soil mix (see later on) to the raised bed and planted it on top of the clay. Over time, the clay would have broken down as worms took the good soil from the raised bed down into the heavy clay.

Raised beds have many advantages, including:

• Fewer weeds – as you typically use a special soil mix that doesn't get compacted because you do not walk on it, there are fewer weeds plus they are easier to pull out. You can also more densely plant a raised bed, which tends to crowd out the weeds and prevent them from getting established. As you are using clean soil, there are no weed seeds in the soil to compete with your vegetables

• Better water retention in sandy soils – as you are putting a special soil mix in the raised bed, it will be better than your sandy soil, particularly if you use the recommended soil mixes. If your soil is sandy, then you can add organic matter, sphagnum moss, or vermiculite to help it retain water and not dry out so quick

• Better draining in clay soils – amending a clay soil is very difficult and a lot of hard work, so building raised beds and filling them with the recommended soil mix means you can plant a wider variety of crops on your plot without having to worry about the clay soil killing your plants

• Greater growing space – because you use a special soil mix you can plant more densely than you can in normal soil, which means you get more out of the same area of ground. Yes, you have space for paths between the raised beds, but that means your plants are protected from accidental damage, and it is easier for you to get around your plot, particularly during bad weather

- Better for your back – if you struggle to bend then a raised bed can be built as high as you need so that you do not need to spend a lot of time bending

- Ideal for wheelchair gardeners – if you are in a wheelchair and want to garden then raised beds are ideal because you can build them so they can be reached from your wheelchair. When built the right height and width, the entire vegetable garden can be managed from your wheelchair

- No dig gardening – as the soil isn't compacted by human feet it remains loose, meaning no heavy digging in the autumn/spring before planting. This will make your gardening friends very jealous and help protect your back as you don't need to dig

- Allows for earlier planting – raised beds warm quicker in the spring and are much easier to protect from the cold, which means you can start planting earlier than you could in the soil. They are easy to fleece, particularly if the soil level is below the top of the bed or you can easily build a frame for fleece or polythene to keep the bed warm

- Longer growing season – for the same reason, raised beds to stay warm for longer, meaning you extend your growing season and get more out of your plot.

- Easy to protect from frost – raised beds are very easy to cover either with fleece, polythene, or glass if there is a cold snap and you need to protect your seedlings. This makes it much easier to deal with an early or late frost, so you don't lose any of your plants

- Easy pH adjustment – you can easily adjust the pH level of a raised bed depending on what you are planting, and it will not affect other plants, which it can do when adjusting the pH without a raised bed. I have a raised bed that is full of ericaceous compost in which I grow blueberries – the acid soil the blueberries love does not affect the rest of my vegetable garden

- Less soil erosion – because the beds are framed, and the paths tend to be covered in something like bark or weed membrane, you find that your vegetable garden doesn't suffer from soil erosion and is generally much neater

- Prevents waterlogged roots – if you have a high water table or live in a wet area then the roots of your plants can get waterlogged, but with a raised bed you can create a free draining soil so that you can grow vegetables without this problem. One end of my vegetable plot would regularly develop large puddles during rain showers, which made it hard to grow anything. Putting in raised beds meant that the puddles formed on the paths and didn't affect the vegetables in the beds which grew quite happily

If your soil is poor quality or even contaminated, then you can put down some plastic sheeting or weed membrane underneath your raised bed. Your plants will only grow in the clean soil you have filled the bed with, not down into the original contaminated soil in your garden.

If you have a dog, which as any gardener will tell you can be a recipe for plant destruction, then building raised beds high enough so the dog can't get into the beds will help to keep the dog out and keep your vegetables safe! However, larger dogs may be more difficult to protect against, but you can still help reduce damage.

The downside of a raised bed is that you need material to build the beds. This can cost a lot, depending on what you are building your beds out of, though you can often find materials cheap or free. Scaffolding boards can be bought second hand for a fraction of their new price and bricks can often be got for free from demolition projects or house renovations. Many people renovating a house will be happy for you to remove their 'waste' as it keeps their costs down. There are plenty of ways for you to build raised beds cheaply and you will find out more about those later in this book.

Another cost will be soil to fill the raised beds, and you aren't going to get away from the cost of compost unless you produce your own. You can usually get horse manure free from anyone who owns a horse and often you can find topsoil free from other people's gardening projects (check Freecycle and similar websites for these offers). The best time to find free soil is spring through to summer when people are undertaking garden projects. It will cost them money to get rid of the soil, but with a trailer or some strong bags, you can take away as much as they have to offer.

Mix the two and you will have soil that will be okay for a raised bed if you let the manure rot down. Horse manure ideally needs ten to twelve months to rot down fully. However, fill the bed with manure, add some worms (dig them up), and then cover with black plastic and the manure can break down in half that time. If you are on a tight budget, then this is the best way to do it and to also start composting yourself (see my How to Compost book for more information) and use that in future years. If you run a hot compost heap, which takes regular work, then you can produce fresh compost in a couple of months.

Raised beds make gardening neater and more convenient. In my raised beds I am growing on soil that I would otherwise struggle to grow on because of the rocks under it. Some of my beds are on top of an old road and so long as I don't plant deep rooted crops, this area is perfectly usable rather than a potential wasteland. I am finding crop rotation to be incredibly easy because I know exactly where things have been planted and a bed typically contains just one type of plant or plants from the same family, e.g. salad plants. Also, for someone of my limited artistic abilities, drawing rectangles on paper for planning is something I can manage.

Once raised beds are built, they will last for years, and if you use bricks, they can become permanent structures. Even with wood though, a raised bed will last for anywhere from four to ten years, depending on the type of wood you use. They are definitely worth the investment, and you will certainly get your money's worth, and it removes some of the hard work.

All in all raised beds will make your gardening easier. It will help you know where your crops are, avoid accidental damage and give your plants the best possible soil. As you read this book, you will find out more about raised beds and how to create your very own raised bed garden. There are a lot of benefits to raised beds, and I hope you enjoy yours as much as I enjoy mine.

PLANNING AND LOCATING YOUR RAISED BED GARDEN

One of the main premises of raised beds is that you do not stand on the soil and that you can reach any point in the raised bed from the outside. Therefore, your first consideration when building a raised bed is to consider how far you can reach. Typically, a raised bed will be no more than four feet wide which assumes a comfortable reach of two feet. The length of your raised bed will vary depending on how you are planning to set out the beds. Paths between raised beds are typically wide enough for a wheelbarrow, so around 18 to 24 inches wide. You may, of course, adjust this width depending on your individual needs so if you are a wheelchair user, then your paths may well be wider to accommodate your wheelchair.

Firstly, draw out your vegetable plot to scale on a piece of paper before you start buying materials so you can plan out exactly what you need. Then draw in raised beds with paths between them, so you maximize the use of your space.

A lot of people find that raised beds of 4' x 6' are a good size because you can reach anywhere in the bed and it is big enough for most vegetables. On my plot, most of the beds are this size though there are some, built by the old occupant I hasten to add, that are larger. A couple is 6' x 6' and one is 6' x 10', which requires a degree of acrobatics to avoid compacting the soil!

It depends on your available space as to how you design your beds. If you are building your beds against a fence, for example, you may design the bed to be two or three feet deep but run the entire length of the fence as there is no need to break it up with paths because it is against a fence. Also as you cannot get around to the other side of the bed, because of the fence, your bed will be half the width.

When designing your raised beds, you need to take into consideration the path the sun takes across your garden. Be careful that you do not plant taller plants so that they shade smaller plants (unless you are protecting the smaller plants from direct sun). Also, ensure that you don't build tall raised beds that then shade lower ones either.

Planning Your Raised Beds

Once you have the best layout for your raised beds, you then need to calculate the materials that you need. As your diagram is to scale it is very easy because you can measure the sizes of the raised bed and calculate the required wood/bricks from that. You can even work out the volume of soil required by multiplying together the length, width and required height of the soil. So, if your bed was 4' x 6' and you wanted the soil 1' deep, then your calculation would be 4 x 6 x 1 or 24 cubic feet of soil.

WHERE TO PLANT

You must match the right plants with the right position on the raised bed. If your garden is a small one, you might not have enough options to make do with as regards space, but there are a variety of plants that can suit different aspects and portions of the garden – be it the shady area or the damp environment or even dry soil. All you have to is to locate the best plant that will fit into the particular space.

Shady Corners of your garden

Plants in general require sunlight for their metabolism and production of food. It is also necessary that they get enough of it to grow. If your little garden is located in such an environment that it receives little or no sunlight, then you don't have to despair. There are other plant options you can plant in those spaces. Some plants are shade loving. You can utilize them for this space. Some of these plants include leafy crops such as cabbage, spinach, and summer salads. All of these plants prefer a cool environment so shades are going for them. Their beds will hardly go dry because of the available shade. This will allow the root system to enjoy enough cool temperature. Some other ornamental crops such as hostas, ferns, epimediums, and hellebores are known to thrive in shady corners of the garden.

Observe the light trajectory

Before constructing a raised bed, one of such things that I put into consideration is the direction of the sunlight and how space accommodates it. This is necessary particularly in small gardens that fall in between walls. Note that some plants that are still growing can possibly grow out of the sunlight once they have reached a certain height. Also, taller plants can suddenly block an area and hinder its reception of sunlight.

You should make a study of your compound and find out where the sunlight rests most time of the day. Raised beds that are constructed in such spaces will naturally be warmer and sunnier because of the constant sunlight they are receiving. This is ideal because each raised bed should receive as much sunlight as possible.

Don't only consider places that have the most sunlight alone. Also, put into consideration the spacing of the sun-filled location. Look for the largest space in your compound where the sun rests the most. While doing this, put the current weather condition into consideration. Remember that the sun is much higher in summer than in autumn and winter. If you are hoping to extend the season, do check to see whether your garden still receives sunlight when it is at its lowest height.

To let in more light into the garden, you can cut back overhanging and overgrown vegetation and branches. If you have neighbors who have trees in their gardens that have overgrown and have started affecting the light reception in your garden, you ask them to trim it down a little for your sake. Sometimes the height of your fence can also pose a challenge to the reception of sunlight. You can reduce it to allow more sunlight, although this can cost you some of your privacy.

Where to Locate Your Raised Bed Garden

This is one thing I think should put into a lot of consideration when producing your garden. You should try as much as possible to locate the garden very close to the kitchen if it is a garden that will hold vegetables or other herbs. I have found out that this helps me to be able to easily dash in and out of the kitchen and plug one or two veggies. Also, you should consider your privacy from your neighbors. I once raised the height of my garden bed boundaries to achieve the privacy effect. You can either do that or place the bed on a patio or on a seating bed. If you are going to be planting high trees in your garden, it is best to keep those trees far from the window so they don't block your view of the garden.

Providing Shelter from Elemental Forces

Plants too need some form of shelter and protection from the elements. When plants are exposed to too much wind, you will notice that they decimate and begin to fall off because it causes plants to dry off and it sucks moisture off the ground.

Plants hardly get pollinated in strong winds because most insects that facilitate pollination cannot withstand the strong winds. Whenever I am planting vegetables, I try to provide them with enough protection from the wind. I surround them with hedges, walls, and fences to keep the winds out. I have discovered that the best kind of windbreakers is hedging, but it is semi permeable being that it allows some form of wind circulation.

The other form of wind breakers such as fences can totally prevent wind from getting to the plants, but they can sometimes be dangerous in that excessively strong winds can buffer along the top edge and drop down onto the raised bed with extra force.

WHEN TO PLANT?

This question is an important one. Your answer will be determined by your choice of plants, the current climate within your region, and at what level you choose to do your planting. Some plants thrive in cold weather; broccoli, for example; but tomatoes will die out in such cold temperatures. With each plant, there are the best times to plant them. You must do your research and put down frost dates and take note of soil temperatures. Under no condition should you grow any plant that is averse to cold when the frost hasn't passed?

As some plants are opposed to low temperatures, so are others that can't survive in extreme temperatures. Be careful to figure out what your garden choices may require. On average, most plants do well in reasonable soil temperatures of between sixty to seventy degrees Fahrenheit. In the event where you embark on transplanting, it is vital that you do so when temperatures are average, and the weather is just right. In the case where you transplant and the weather turns out to be harsh, then you'll have to cover them up and shield them from intense sunlight and dry winds.

SITE PREPARATION

One of the questions most frequently asked about raised beds for growing vegetables is just how tall they should be. There is no definite answer to this question, I am afraid. There is no 'ideal height'; it is completely up to the individual. However, there are certain considerations that you must keep in mind. These include the soil conditions under the beds, the costs involved, the depth of the soil required for your specific crop and of course, which height would allow you to work comfortably in your raised beds. This last aspect should take priority if you are a mature gardener.

PREPARATION OF THE GROUND

Double Dig

Although the plants in your raised beds will be provided with their own rich soil, some of them may grow roots that extend into the soil underneath the beds to search for additional nutrients and moisture. Therefore, it is important to prepare the soil below by double digging it. This must be done before you start on your raised beds and once done, need not be repeated.

Double digging simply means the depth to which you have to dig up the soil; it is approximately twenty-four inches deep, or in other words, two lengths of the blade of your shovel. Remove all the hard rocks and debris that could obstruct roots from growing down into the ground. Keep your eyes open for other large roots entering into this space. For instance, trees that grow nearby can send their roots to more than fifty feet diagonally underneath the surface searching for nutrients and water. Double digging will provide an extended reservoir of water and nutrients, which your plants' sturdier, deeper roots can have access.

Digging up the ground also allows you to have a closer look at the status of the underlying soil, and to decide which amendments should be made. If it resembles clay, for instance, peat should be used to lighten it to aerate it and improve the drainage.

Improving the Subsoil

You have cleared the ground area of debris and rock and finished your double digging. If needed, you can now add some peat moss that will lighten your soil. Because peat has an acidic nature, you have to balance the pH level of the soil by adding lime. Sprinkle some rock phosphate over the plot and mix in with the soil. Your ground area is now ready for the raised plant bed, so assemble the frames and fill them up with rich soil. When you almost reach the top of the raised bed, add compost and fertilizer. Do not add the compost and fertilizer too long before the season to avoid early, unexpected spring rainfalls to flush them too far down into your soil.

Consider Drainage

Raised beds have an aesthetic appeal, which speaks to many gardeners, but they also allow for proper drainage of the soil in which your veggies will be grown. In general, most raised beds are eleven inches tall, which is equal to that of two 2 by 6 standard boards. (In actual fact the measurements are 1.5 by 5.5 inches.) The reason why this height is most popular is that it provides adequate drainage for the majority of crops. The best results can be achieved if you allow for another twelve inches at least of rich soil underneath your raised bed. That will give your veggie plants up to twenty inches of good soil. Remember that raised beds usually end up not filled to the brim with soil; after every watering the soil will compress somewhat. You will need this extra space later to add some mulch.

Two factors contribute to the earlier warming up of the soil in raised beds during the spring: Firstly, the soil is always well above the ground level and the second aspect is the good drainage in these beds. Gardeners can therefore start transplanting much earlier and so lengthen the growing season of their veggies. To shield the young, vulnerable seedlings from a late frost or strong winds, place cold frames over the beds. Once the seedlings are stronger and better established, these frames can simply be removed and used elsewhere if needed.

Consider Bending Down

Young gardeners who are fit and energetic might not even waste time thinking about this aspect since going on your knees or bending down to attend to your plants is easy and you take it in your stride. People who suffer from backache or strain or those whose mobility has been impaired will need higher raised beds to help lighten their gardening chores. Beds can be in a range of eight to twenty-four inches high. You will quickly notice the huge difference between tending these various beds. Taller beds are just so much more comfortable when you have to set in transplants, till the soil, weed, and harvest. It is not necessary to put extras strain on your back at all.

Cross Supports for Taller Beds

It is commonsense that taller beds will hold more volume so you have to keep this in mind when you construct a raised bed that is taller than twelve inches, (especially if it is longer than five feet). As mentioned before, after a little watering, the soil will compact slightly, becoming heavier and the pressure may well cause your beds to bulge out on the sides in mid-span. So for beds of this height, you will require cross supports. Place them in the middle of the span, right across the width. This will prevent the two sides from bulging out. If you purchased your raised beds from a garden center these supports were probably included in the package but if your raised beds are home-made, you will have to make your own, using composite plastic, aluminum, or wood.

Soil Depth for Most Vegetables

The Roots Need Adequate Depth

Most nutrients in garden beds are to be found in the top six inches of the soil. The reason is that most vegetable root growth happens in this shallow depth. The key nutrients like fertilizers and compost are added from the top and then tilled in lightly. Mulches also are applied on the top surfaces of the beds from time to time; they eventually decompose to add extra nutrients to the soil, enriching it.

If moisture and nutrients are available deeper in the soil, tap roots will grow down to reach them. This brings additional trace minerals to the vegetable plants as well. The larger the plant, the deeper the roots will travel. Deeper roots anchor the plant much firmer into the bed, enabling it to withstand strong winds or heavy rains and saturated soil. Plants with big leaves and shallow root systems like broccoli, cauliflower, and Brussels sprouts will need staking to make sure they do not fall over as they develop and reach maturity.

Do some research before you prepare the raised beds for your upcoming garden since the root depth of different vegetables can vary considerably. This will determine where you plant certain veggies and to what depth the soil needs to be prepared.

Raised beds that have been set on a gravel surface or a concrete patio will not allow roots to grow any deeper down than the depth of the beds. In this case, make sure you know the depth requirements for the different crops. You can compensate for an impenetrable ground surface by making the beds higher, providing enough root space.

The average raised bed is between eight and twelve inches tall, but experienced gardeners have planted in beds with sides exceeding three feet. While these beds are ideal for crops with deep roots, you have to provide good drainage by drilling a number of holes towards the bottom of your beds, right along the sides.

The Height of Mature Vegetables

Tall Plants Blocking Sunlight

Plants are dependent on sunlight for their growth. Plan the layout of your raised garden beds so that they benefit as much as possible from sunlight throughout the day. You have to orientate them in such a way that they will enjoy the maximum amount of sun exposure. Your beds should therefore be arranged to all face in a southerly direction, placing them horizontally one after the next. As the sunlight moves from the east to the west, optimum exposure will be able across all the beds from side to side. Furthermore, this placing will prevent taller plants from blocking the sunlight that their adjacent neighbors need.

I am sure you have seen garden layouts running north-south, in other words, vertically. Some gardeners reason that this arrangement will minimize the possibility of one plant shading another. This may work effectively if you want to grow different varieties of vegetables in the same raised bed. The tallest plants should then be located at the northern side or rear end with the shorter ones in front of them.

No matter how you decide to arrange the raised beds in your garden, it is still important to establish the eventual height of your mature plants to make sure every single one of them will receive the sunlight it needs to flourish and grow to its full potential. On the front or south side, you can plant veggies like radishes and lettuce, following by medium size plants. The tallest vegetable plants will make up the rear or north side of your bed. Remember that those veggies that need trellises like peas and pole beans can easily block out most of the sunlight, so take care where you place them in your bed.

Wind may damage tall plants; their height makes them more vulnerable so they will have to be safely secured to trellises. You will be wise to place them next to a windbreak.

A strong, well-developed root system will provide your plant with the nutrients and moisture it needs to produce the best fruit. If you understand the basic factors about the root systems of your plants; their depth requirements and behavior, you will surely be able to provide them with the ideal conditions for maximum growth and bountiful harvests.

Every successful gardener will tell you that soil preparation comes first when you aim for a bountiful harvest. Without proper soil, you may as well throw in the towel before you even begin. Initially, you should focus all your attention on the condition and quality of soil you are going to use. Good quality soil will ensure that your vegetable plants grow to their full potential and that you will not spend too much valuable time fighting pests and weeds. Following are a few tips for mixing rich and fertile soil to suit all your planters and garden beds. Your locality may influence the type of soil you will need to a small degree, but these basic principles are applicable everywhere, regardless of where you live.

1.   Topsoil does not Always Contain Organic Matter

Purchased soil often looks quite promising: dark in color, well screened, and clean. This might not always be an indication of what it contains. It may well be a good growing medium though without any of the vital organic matter that is essential for growth. Therefore, you should always inquire from the attendant at the garden center what the soil consists of and what its origin is. You should assume that some extra feeding would be necessary to build up this soil to the standards needed for successful gardening.

2.   Revitalize Soil Annually

Usually, new gardens will do fairly well during their initial year even though no additional matter was added to amend the soil. The reason for this is that the available nutrients, organic matter, and trace minerals have not been tapped yet. However, after one or two seasons of successive gardening, the crops will have used up all the riches in the soil. That is why it is so important that you revitalize your gardening soil regularly.

A wonderful solution is to plant 'green manure' as a cover crop after the first two seasons

of growing vegetables. These crops are very easy and simple to grow and have many benefits. As soon as the cover crop has matured, chop it up and then dig it lightly into your soil. Now your soil has been replenished with fresh organic matter. Consider growing leguminous crops like alfalfa or fenugreek since they will fix the atmospheric nitrogen in such a way that it can be used as nutrients by the plants. This type of green manure has many benefits; its roots will loosen the soil, bringing the deeper nutrients nearer to the surface of your garden beds. While you chop up the manure and work it into the ground as well as the activity of the roots will aerate your soil, thus improving the drainage for future crops.

3.   The Soil must be Crumbly, Fluffy, and Light

You want to make it as easy as possible for the roots of your plants to be able to work their way through the layers of soil in search of moisture and nutrients. Compacted and dense soil will make this essential task of plant roots very difficult, and they will spend so much energy struggling to get to the nutrients that not much will be left for the rest of the plant to grow. You can easily facilitate better root growth by lightening your garden soil. This is turn will lead to better vegetative growth and you will see positive results when your plants start to flourish.

How do you know if your soil is light enough? A simple test is to push your finger into it. You should have no trouble to poking it in up to the third knuckle of the finger. If you struggle to achieve this, then you will have to lighten the soil by adding peat moss and working it into the top layer. I have already mentioned that peat moss is acidic by nature, so you will most probably have to add lime. Always enquire about the pH level of the soil you purchase. You need to know if lime will be necessary. Acidic soil is commonly found in most areas of our Country, so lime is usually needed, although there are regions that have alkaline soil. Many gardeners prefer to use vermiculite for lightening the soil because it does not break down at the same speedy rate as the peat moss.

4.   The Ultimate Amendment for Soil: Compost

Making your own compost is easy and can save you extra expense. Many gardeners have a compost heap in their back gardens. Compost consists of organic material filled with nutrients to turn normal soil into a rich medium for all your plants. Use this valuable resource correctly and wisely and you can be sure of a prolific vegetable garden. Instead of adding compost to the soil right after harvesting, rather postpone it to two or three weeks before you plant your next crop. You want to prevent a sudden downpour from washing away all that wonderful richness in the compost and undo all your hard work.

The general idea amongst many people who consider a compost heap an unsightly, smelly mess is truly a misconception. If you go about, it the correct way, your compost heap will be neat and tidy with a wonderfully rich and earthy aroma. Veteran gardeners will tell you that active compost heaps should not be smelly. If your plot is too small to allow for a larger compost pile, you can purchase a sealed composter. This device contains smells and is small and tidy in appearance. Because they are sealed, they are immune to dogs, mice, raccoons, and such-like critters.

A composter in your garden has an additional benefit; it will take care of all the dead plant matter left after the harvest. After your last tomatoes have been harvested, carefully remove all the 'skeletons' from the plants, break or chop them into smaller pieces and simply throw them into the compost pile. It is a wonderful way to re-use all plant residues in your garden to contribute to the nutrient-rich compost for your future crops. Just inspect the dead plant matter carefully for any diseases before you add it to the composter.

5.   Organic Fertilizers are the Best Choice

Do not be overly enticed by all the many product claims you read on the packaging of chemical fertilizers. They may be true, but the advantages often do not last and are rather short-lived. You will have to reapply them regularly after each planting. In the end, the benefits of these commercial fertilizers may be lessened to some extent because they do not improve the condition of the soil, the most important aspect of successful gardening. I would therefore suggest that when you find yourself short of compost, make use of organic fertilizer. It will also give your little seedlings an instant boost. Canola meal is one of the popular fertilizers. This material is finely ground and lightweight, making it very easy to sprinkle onto your beds. On top of that, it is relatively inexpensive and free of weeds. (Some kinds of manures may include weeds). Make sure to mix the canola meal lightly into the topsoil because mice love it and may attack your beds. For the same reason, take care where you store your bag. It should be well sealed and in any dry spot where mice will not be able to reach.

CHAPTER 2. HOW TO BUILD A RAISED BED GARDEN

People who have been gardening for a very long time use raised beds to avoid an array of gardening challenges. In fact, gardening in raised beds is so easy that a beginner can do it.

You can get rid of the bad dirt because you control the soil and compost blend you put into your raised bed garden. You build drainage into the walls, which still holds the soil and keeps erosion from happening. Raised beds get more sun exposure, which means that it gets warmer and allows for more diversity in the plants and a longer growing season. You can place the plants closer together, therefore you yield more, weeds are crowded out, and water use is maximized. Also, raising the soil level even just twelve inches- one foot- greatly reduces the back breaking effort of planting, weeding, and harvesting.

Raised bed gardens are a dream come true for a gardener. With all those positives, what is not to love about them? While building a raised bed garden isn't all that complicated, here are the steps you need to take to make your own raised bed garden.

1) Before you can get started, you must figure out how big you want your raised bed to be. If you're not sure how big you want it to be, then you should first start with a four-by-four foot square, which is the distance that most people can reach the middle from either side. Then, you will want to level the ground so that your raised bed will be completely flat.

A raised bed that is three by six will be wide enough to support tomatoes, but yet still narrow enough that you can reach it from both sides. Ideally, you want to make it one to two feet tall. You can make it taller, but keep in mind that the bigger you make it, the more soil you will need.

Make sure that you find a fairly flat spot. It will save you a lot of time and effort in the preparation process. After all, you want your walls to be level, right? As far as placement, the general rule is that a North-South placement can take advantage of the available light all day long. Try to avoid areas that are shaded by the house or by trees. Besides, if building multiple beds, you will want to leave at least eighteen inches between so that you can walk through, or if you will need room for a lawnmower or wheel barrow, leave two feet.

2) Make your walls. To start, get 4 one-foot long four by fours to create the corner posts, 8 four-foot long two by sixes for the side rails, and 4 two-foot long two by twos for the center stakes.

Put your four by fours on each corner of the area you marked off. Starting with all of your choices, screw in your first two by six to secure the corners together. Stack another two by six on top of the first. Make sure that your ends are even with the ends of the posts. You can use an angle-square to be sure that the rails and posts are lined up correctly.

You will want to build the walls separately then fasten them together before putting the raised bed into position. Placing the corner posts and posts halfway along the walls offers stability for your raised bed, so you want to do this. They will also help to hold your bed in place and reduce the pressure that the soil will exert on your frame. You can use a cap railing around the top of the frame to tie it all together and offer you a great place to lay down your tools while you are working or sit and admire your handiwork. You can get bed covers to keep insects away and keep your plants warm in the cooler weather.

These instructions use wood to create the raised beds. You can use bricks if you wish or you can use wood to create frames and then use sheet metal for the walls. There will be more on that later on. You should remember that if you are using lumber, you need to use wood that has not been persevered with toxins. Make sure to stay away from creosote railroad ties- instead choose cedar or redwood, which is naturally rot resistant. Another option is ACQ (alkaline copper quaternary) treated wood, it is safe for food crops. However, you might want to consider using landscape fabric between it and the soil to keep them from coming in contact. Use galvanized or stainless screws or bolts to put them together, regardless of the type of wood you use.

3) Connect the walls together. You will now stand the sidewalls up and opposite each other with the corner posts on the outside.

4) Now, you want to square it up. To do this, you will measure diagonally in both directions across the planter to make sure the frame is exactly square. Adjust your raised bed until both diagonals are equal lengths.

5) Make your walls sturdy. Take the two-by-two stakes and place them in the middle of each of the outside walls, and pound it into the ground so that the top of the stake is level with the top of the wall.

6) Fill your raised bed with topsoil. Once your bed is complete, it is time to fill it. You will want to use quality topsoil, especially if your natural ground isn't conducive to plant growth. You may also want to add organic materials such as peat moss or compost. After you have done all this and watered the soil well, it's time to start planting your plants.

Make sure that you don't get soil from the ground- especially if your natural ground isn't conducive to growing plants. Use compost, a soil mix, or even peat moss for your raised beds. You will want to use a two by four to level out the soil and then you can plant. If space allows, consider building more than one bed, which will make life much easier- you can rotate crops and make sure that you can meet the watering needs of each individual type of plant. If you line up the beds in rows, you simplify the process of installing an irrigation system.

7) You can create a framework for a lightweight cover with hoops and extend the growing season in the cooler areas, conserve moisture in the drier areas, and protect plants from insects or birds. To do this, you will use galvanized pipes to mount one-inch PVC pipes inside of the raised bed walls. Then, cut ½-inch flexible PVC tube that is twice the width of the bed, bend it, mount it, and attach it. You should use a clear film to raise the air and soil temperatures in the early fall or spring to help you get an early start on planting. Be careful that you don't bake your plants on the warmer days. To avoid excess heat buildup, you will want to either remove the cover or cut slits in it. To control pests, cover the bed with row covers, which are a gauzelike fabric, or bird netting. These will let in the air and the light, but keep out the flying insects.

As was mentioned before, you can find pre-made, boxed raised garden beds, so you don't have to go to the hassle of making your own. If you do want to make your own, you can make it as large or as small as you like. You can make it square, rectangle, hexagonal, basically any shape you can think of- as long as it has straight sides (it would be a little difficult to make a round one, but you could try).

PLANTING YOUR RAISED BED GARDEN

If your soil is extremely compacted or has poor drainage, it can be very difficult to have a garden- but we all want to eat more fruits and vegetables, right? If you have the problem of poor soil, then raised bed gardening is your best option.

They take a small amount of space, and you can build them on a concrete patio. The drainage provided in a raised bed is greater than that of an in-ground garden. A raised bed that is 1 foot in depth provides sufficient room for most roots.

If your bed is narrow, about 3 feet or less, you won't have to step on the soil, which means the soil won't get compacted. Plants grow much better in loose soil.

Be sure that you don't build your raised bed on a wooden deck. Once the bed is full of water and soil, the weight could cause damage to the structure.

If the bed will be sitting on the ground, be sure to line the bed with chicken wire or hardware cloth to prevent burrowing animals (moles & gophers) from coming up into your garden.

As mentioned before, your raised garden bed can be made of a wide variety of materials. You can build it from stone, cinderblocks, wood, brick, or any other material that you can build a base that is at least 1 foot deep. You will want to choose a location in your yard that gets a minimum of six hours of sunlight every day. You can raise almost any type of vegetable in a raised bed. The only thing that doesn't grow well is potatoes and corn. The potatoes need lots of room for their roots and the corn would be so high it would be hard to harvest it.

Timber Raised Bed

The construction of a timber raised bed is fairly simple and straightforward. First of all, level and mark out the area where you would like your raised bed to be. Bear in mind that it should not be under overhanging trees, and in an area where you can have easy access for tending your plants. It should get a minimum of 5-6 hours of sunshine per day to produce the best results for most vegetables.

For a 6 x 3 x 1.5 foot bed built using traditional decking timber, (I tend to use decking as it is stronger than just plain boards) you will need:

6 lengths decking @ 6' x 6" x 1"

6 lengths decking @ 2'10" x 6" x 1"

10 – 3" x 2" pointed posts @ 30"

Weed control fabric

Galvanized screws or nails

Wire mesh (optional)

Although the following instructions are aimed at an 'anchored' bed, it is also acceptable to simply make the corner posts the same depth as the bed itself, and lay the whole frame on the ground – the weight of soil will usually keep it anchored in place. Begin by marking out with string and pegs, the area of your raised bed, putting down a peg on each corner. This is where you should consider whether or not you are going to dig out any of the existing ground.

Questions to ask you are, what depth of compost do I need, versus what height do I want the finished bed to be. If you are growing root vegetables that need depth, but you do not want the finished height to be over 1 foot for instance, then digging out the area to the depth required is your only option. This 'digging out' however may not be necessary if you have good quality topsoil. Simply loosen the existing soil with a garden fork and add your infill mix (more on this later) to the required level.

Once this decision is made, then we can proceed with building the raised bed. Once you have the pegs in the area that marks out the four corners of your raised bed, you simply take out one peg at a time and replace it by hammering down your pointed posts, leaving

them a minimum of 18 inches above the ground.

Alternatively, if you make these posts longer then you can use them as handy aids for lifting yourself when tending your vegetables – just a matter of choice.

The best way to do this is to put down one post at the end, then temporarily fix the first short end against the post. With this done, then hammer in the second post flush with the end of the 6" x 2" decking plank. Proceed with the two longer sides, then complete the other end. If you just put one screw partially home, then you can easily adjust it to suit.

Be sure that you have leveled the timber and that you have left a minimum 12" in height above the first planks, so you are able to complete the job.

I find that it is better to construct with a cordless screwdriver as this does not impact the framework in the same way that hammer, and nails do. Also, should you make a slight error, then it is no trouble to take apart for adjustment.

Once this is done then simply mark out along the inside length two feet from each end, then making sure the construction is straight, hammer in two of the posts to the same height as the others. At the end of the construction, do the same with one post in the center of the framework.

This will give you a strong sturdy construction, which you will need if you do not want the sides of your raised deck to bow under the pressure of the soil.

Point of note:

If you are building with heavier timbers, say 6" x 2" for instance then it may be possible to just put one post in the center of the long side and none at all on the end. I however tend to lean on the cautious side, and would rather aim for a stronger option overall. Another tip is to put a cross brace in if you are concerned about the sides bowing outward. After you have built the sides then just screw down the remaining planking face down along the edge (as in the photograph), to make a comfortable sitting or leaning area for tending to your raised bed.

One thing to consider during this time is whether or not you are bothered by Gophers or Moles. If you are, then at this point you would place in 1" galvanized wire mesh, covering the bottom of your raised bed. This will be extremely effective in stopping the varmints from destroying your crop and giving you endless grief and heartache!

The weed control fabric should be fixed down the inside of the bed, to keep the wet soil away from the timber. This will help the timber to breathe and make it just that bit longer lasting.

2nd Point of note: Do not use timber that has been treated with creosote, as this may weep through and kill the plants!

If you think you may wish to move them to another location perhaps in the next season, then it is probably best not to hammer the corner posts into the ground and instead make them the actual height of the bed itself.

In other words, your 18 inch high bed will just need 18 inch high posts instead of 30 inches or so. These will be fixed in the same way as the corner posts and the infill will hold the whole construction in place – though not as well as the former method!

Here is an example of a larger construction 9 foot in length and 18 inches high. As you can see, this bed is built to sit upon a concrete base. Built with three rows of decking, it has 2 center braces made from 3 x 2 to keep it solid.

Possibly the simplest form of Raised Bed is the 4 foot square model. This can be constructed from decking material by simply adding a short corner post at each corner and fixing it together with decking screws. Everything else is constructed the same way as the larger deck.

Materials needed would be ..

2 lengths decking @ 4' x 6" x 1"

2 lengths decking @ 3'10" x 6" x 1"

4 – 2" x 2" pointed posts @ 18"

Weed control fabric

Galvanized screws or nails

Wire mesh (optional)

Again, you have the option to simply use 6 inch posts at the corners if you have no need to 'lock in' to the ground area.

To create a 'Square Foot Garden then simply add a 'grid' as in the picture below using garden canes or even twine to mark out the foot-square areas for planting.

Regarding Timber: Some people have concerns over whether or not to use treated or untreated timber to build their Raised Beds. This is perfectly understandable as more of us

become aware of the possibility of contamination regarding chemicals that have been used to treat the timbers.

There are 2 main issues to consider here, and that is the effect that treated timber may have on the plants themselves. And the effect that may be had as the consumer of these same vegetables – if indeed they survive!

Modern timber treatment via tanalisation methods according to the soil association (www.soilassociation.org) is perfectly suitable for garden structures such as Raised Beds or compost bins – provided the timber has been purchased already treated.

Various blogs will insist that there could be an issue with the chemicals leaching out of the timber, but I have found no evidence for this – although I do agree that it is unwise to use treated timber sawdust in the compost for instance and that I would not use it on the barbeque where toxins could be released into the atmosphere – and your food!

'Old' methods such as the creosote that would be used on timber railway sleepers however are definitely hazardous to the plants themselves and should be avoided for any planting constructions – unless it is covered or lined with a suitable polythene membrane. I recommend lining timber Raised Beds anyway as this reduces water leakage and lengthens the life of the timbers.

If the plants' foliage comes into contact with creosote then it will wither and die, simple as that.

To sum-up. As far as I can deduct there is no real evidence to show that plants grown in treated timber structures, do in any way absorbs the chemicals that have been used to treat the timber.

However – If in doubt simply use untreated timber or line with polythene membrane. Even an untreated timber bed will still give you at least 5-7 years of use before it starts to decay.

CONCRETE BLOCK RAISED BED

Like the earlier construction, this is made from concrete block, laid flat; this is a simple construction that can be taken down when and if, it's not needed any longer. Owing to the pure weight of the block however, it is far stronger than the dry-laid brick model.

If you use 18" x 9" x 4" dense block, then layout a flat area for the base, pounding in some crushed rock for a foundation. After making sure your foundation track is perfectly level, using a straight edge; Start to lay your block on the flat side down on a bed of rough sand. This row must be perfectly level otherwise you will face problems as the structure rises. Make sure that you overlap the blocks so that there is no break going up through the wall. The down side with this raised bed is that you will use twice the concrete block as building normally, however you will save on sand and cement as well as time.

Drywall Example Above

The finished result should be a solid construction that has a good broad top to sit on while working for your raised bed. True, it takes up a bit more space, but overall it is perhaps the simplest and quickest way to build. Just be sure of the first layer, and everything else will follow on.

Be sure that you tie in the corners using the same building method, overlapping the blocks at the corners as well as the sides.

Top Tip: If you would like a more secure finish, then simply lay the top row of the block on a bed of cement mortar. This will secure the whole structure quite nicely.

SQUARE FOOT BED

Another interesting idea for a raised bed garden is to follow the principle of the 'square foot' gardening method. Square foot gardening is simply taking a structure of four foot by four foot, and separating them into one foot squares by means of a simple framework placed over the top of the area. This can be done with canes as in the above example, strips of timber, or taught nylon string.

This gives sixteen potential 'mini plots' to work with. The idea here is that a family of four can produce enough vegetables throughout the growing season to feed them all comfortably and cheaply.

Unbelievable as this may sound, it is indeed possible if enough thought has gone into the preparation and a good rotational plan is followed. One of the good things about this plan (and there are many) is that the plot should never need to be artificially fertilized as the vegetables in each plot take only the nutrients that they need, and as they move around they leave the other nutrients for the plants that come along behind.

As an example of this, you have grown beans and peas. They take nitrogen from the air and leave it in the soil. Thus it is good to let these plants die at the end of their growing season and in turn fertilize the soil with a nitrogen rich environment for vegetables such as Cabbage Cauliflower or kale that love this environment.

As in fact do potatoes, though they should not be planted alongside brassicas as they prefer different pH levels.

This is the traditional crop rotation method in miniature and works very well for the four foot square garden.

If we simply take this method and place it into a six by four foot raised bed, then you would have twenty four potential planting areas. This is more than enough for the average family needs of vegetables if it is properly handled.

Hot Bed Raised Bed

An extremely effective way to get an early start with your RBG is to use it as a 'Hot' Bed.

There are 2 main ways to effectively create a hot bed – artificial, with the help of hot water or electricity. Or natural, with the help of decomposing organic material.

Using either of these techniques means a longer growing season as you can start earlier and finish later owing to the warmer nature of the growing medium.

An artificial Hot Bed can be created by laying a special layer of electric cable or blanket about 6-12 inches (150-300mm) below the surface. This depth is largely determined by the root depth of the plant you are growing.

Most soil heating cables are thermostatically set at around 70°F (21°C) although the more expensive models have adjustable thermostats fitted.

Make sure you have an electrical outlet close by. Layout the cable according to the manufacturer's instructions, then cover over with soil – job done!

The electric soil heater technique has the advantage of being quick to fit, and manageable with regard to heat control. However, on the downside is the cost of the electricity – or indeed the supply itself.

An organic Hot Bed is a little more 'manual' but has the advantage in that it does not run up your electric bill, and feeds the crops over a long period – meaning no need for artificial fertilizers.

These organic beds are usually created within a cold-frame or Raised Bed. Either way, in order to work effectively they have to be covered over to preserve the heat generated.

This heat is generated by a layer of fresh manure, preferably horse manure. I emphasize the word 'fresh' If the manure has already decomposed then there will be little or no heat generated, and all you will have is the nutrient benefits of the manure itself.

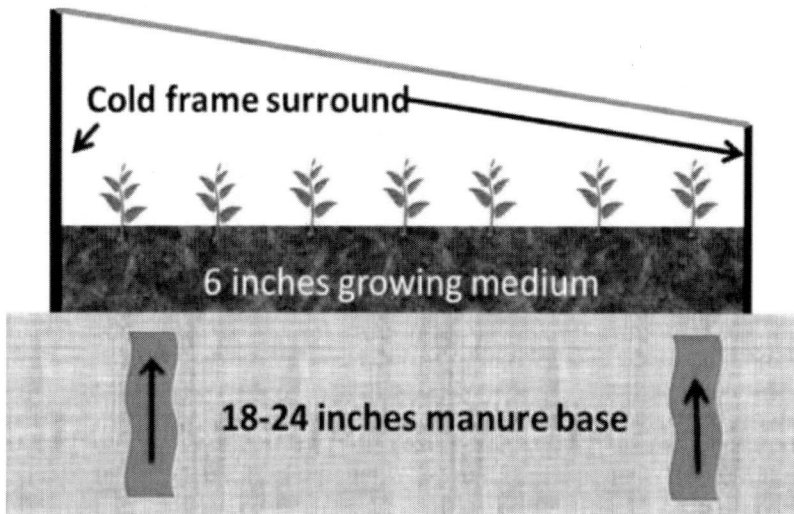

Cold frame surround

6 inches growing medium

18-24 inches manure base

As you may see from the illustration above. Fresh manure is placed in a trench, and the growing medium is layered on top. As the manure begins to decompose it heats up the bed.

The details are simple no matter how you achieve the end goal. After placing the manure in the trench – or the complete base of the frame as in the preceding illustration – trample it down firmly, and soak completely before covering it over with soil.

This will 'kick-start' the decomposition process, and assures you of good results. A compost thermometer is handy in this instance to keep a check on the ground temperature before planting, otherwise, especially in the early stages it may get too hot for the young plants.

The heating aspect of a hot bed of this nature does not last forever – maybe 3-4 months. However, the nutrients produced by the manure will last for many months – even into the next season.

If you have a greenhouse or polytunnel, then a Hot Bed can be very effective over the winter months for keeping the inside temperatures just above freezing. This makes it an effective way to over-winter plants that cannot withstand severe frosts.

The way to achieve this is simply to make a wooden frame and pack in the fresh manure as before, covering lightly with soil. Leave uncovered. This will act as a warm radiator for your polytunnel.

OTHER RAISED BED EXAMPLES

There is actually no limit to the number of ways to construct a raised bed garden area, or indeed the different materials that can be used for it. Or perhaps I should say that the only real limit is your imagination!

Corrugated iron sheeting, properly supported is often used to create a raised bed. It has to be said though that if you are building for appearance, then this is probably not the one for you!

Timber logs cut straight from the tree. These can look especially effective and can be built similar to a log cabin construction, giving an extremely strong and versatile structure that will last for many years.

Old Railway sleepers

I would not particularly recommend using old railway sleepers, as there is a danger of creosote leaking into your plant bed, causing a health hazard – as well as killing the plants. If old sleepers are used then be sure to line the inside with polythene barrier to prevent this happening.

In general, however the modern railway sleepers for sale in your local garden center will not have been treated with creosote, but with a plant-friendly injection treatment. This makes them ideal for raised bed construction. Rot – resistant cedar or redwood are the best railway ties for building your raised bed. Consult the salesperson before purchasing.

Build using the same principles above for the timber raised bed, but because of the heavy timber (about 19" x 5") you need only use support at the corners, except for the long lengths at over 3 meters.

Filled sandbags

Yes, even sandbags can easily be utilized to form a Raised Bed of virtually any size. Simply fill and layer the bags as you would when building a brick wall. This is a quick and simple method to create an effective planting area.

CHAPTER 3: TOP VEGETABLES FOR RAISED BED

Raised bed gardening is becoming more and more popular to take maximum advantage of small spaces. If you plant your raised bed garden correctly, you can get amazing crops of vegetables, flowers, and herbs with very little effort compared to what you must do in traditional gardening.

These types of gardens have an important role in the landscape of the home. They feature framed areas above the ground and often have wooden frames around the area. They have an increased ability to drain away excess water and eliminate compacted soil. In addition, you can add soil nutrients as necessary to help your plants be the best they can be. This allows gardeners to plant a variety of plants in their gardens.

Most plants will work well in raised bed gardens. The exception is those plants that are large or have very deep roots or sprawling top growth. Other plants that don't work in raised beds are those that are top-heavy and tall and therefore need to be firmly anchored. Since the plants in your raised beds will be sharing soil, light, fertilizer, and water, you should make sure to choose plants with similar or the same requirements for growth and development.

As far as size, moderately tall plants work well. Also, trailing plants or smaller plants work quite well in raised bed gardens and can be planted together. Planting in raised beds is just another type of container gardening, and therefore basically requires you to follow the same rules. Plant your tallest plants in the center of your bed, and go down to the smaller plants near the edge. Plant the trailing plants along the edges, so they spill over.

Vegetables are easy to grow in raised beds. You can maximize the amount of yield you get from your crops by planting the summer plants as soon as the spring ones have been harvested and fall ones as soon as the summer ones have been harvested. Since the fertilizer and soil are easier to control, you can plant vegetables and plants closer together than in a traditional garden.

In addition, raised bed gardens are being used to raise tropical houseplants as annuals. In the fall, you can dig them up and bring them in for the winter. The raised garden beds can be a spectacular addition to your backyard décor.

As far as flowering plants go, you can raise both annuals and perennials in your raised garden. You should choose annuals that match the availability of sunlight in your area. Annuals will add a pop of color and look great as border additions in your garden. The growing conditions offered in the raised bed garden seriously increase the growth of the annuals, so make sure that you allow enough room for them to grow. Annuals will flourish in the rich soil offered in the raised bed garden.

Perennials will give your garden a more permanent addition. They will flower year after year and can form the basis for your raised bed garden. You can add perennials to create a low maintenance garden that requires very little work through the seasons. To achieve constant color and flowering, you should choose plants that bloom at various times of the year.

Raised bed gardens are great for vegetable gardening because they offer a neat area for planting. The rich soil will ensure that you have a prosperous harvest, providing that you have placed them in such a way that there is room for growth. Make sure that you read all your labels so that you can decide on the best placement for the plants. An added benefit of the raised bed garden is that it keeps pests out- the frame provides a base to which you can place poles to attach fencing.

PEAS

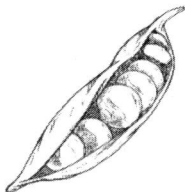

Peas work well in raised garden beds, according to the National Gardening Association. The raised design helps drain the excess water away and allows gardeners to plant earlier. You should plant peas after the last frost of the winter.

PEPPERS

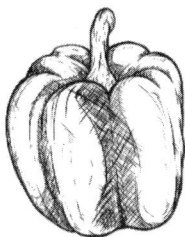

According to the National Gardening Association, peppers grow quite well in raised bed gardens, especially if they're really wet. This is because of the drainage and the warmer temperatures offered by raised bed gardens. It's best to plant them after the last spring frost, but they can be started inside earlier and then moved outside in order to create an earlier harvest.

EGGPLANT

Like peppers, raised beds are great for growing eggplants. They like lots of sun as they grow and will do exceptionally well with a layer of mulch around the base of the plants in order to prevent the growth of weeds. Eggplants have beautiful purple flowers that make your vegetable garden especially attractive.

OKRA

Okra grows quite well in raised beds and does really well next to peppers and eggplants. According to the National Gardening Association, you should plant okra from a seed. It doesn't do well with frost and doesn't do well in a really hot climate either. If you live in an area with a really cold winter, you can still plant okra, provided that your spring and summer months will be warm.

Another great addition to raised bed gardens are herbs. They grow just as well as the vegetables and annuals will. The extra organic material and the soil looseness allow the roots to spread quite nicely. When the roots spread, the plant can better absorb nutrients and moisture from the soil. Herbs can be paired with vegetables or annuals or can be planted all on their own. You should disperse those strong-smelling herbs throughout the garden to repel insects. In addition, you will attract bees and butterflies, which will keep the pests to a minimal level.

TOMATOES

Tomatoes are one of the easier vegetables to grow, but there are still environmental factors you will need to plan for and take into consideration during the spring and summer growing seasons. Growing a full and healthy set of tomatoes is accomplished by considering issues of sun exposure, watering, and soil health.

Location and Soil

Tomato plants like full sun and they always should get several hours of sun a day. Little sun means little tomatoes or even non-producing plants.

If you are growing from seed start them indoors or in a greenhouse about 6 weeks before the last frost. Plant out into garden beds when frosts are over.

Tomatoes enjoy very fertile soil and will respond well to organic matter mixed into the beds. One of the mistakes that new tomato growers often make is watering the plants too much and not giving the soil enough attention. Till about 5 or 6 inches of soil, and mix compost into the area.

Types of Tomatoes

Tomatoes are usually referred to as "hybrids" or "heirlooms," different types of tomatoes offer different benefits. While an heirloom tomato has a long history of tasty tomato production, hybrid tomato plants will usually offer more fruit each season.

Hybrid plants are also usually much more resistant to disease. Certain types of hybrids have even been grown to be resistant to a specific type of disease, which may be helpful for a person with a garden in a disease-prone area.

Watering

A tomato plant should be watered at its base and its best not to get the leaves wet. Unless temperatures reach near 100 degrees during the day, the plants may be watered every 2 or 3 days.

These plants won't tolerate soggy conditions which is another plus for using a raised bed to plant them in. If you set it up properly with the optimum soil profile, then drainage won't be an issue.

CUCUMBERS

Because they are so easy to grow, include cucumbers when you are starting with your raised bed vegetable garden. Most cucumbers are of the vine type and send out runners, but there are also some varieties of bush cucumbers and they generally fall into 2 category types...pickling and slicing cucumbers.

Cucumbers also like soil that is rich in organic matter and is well drained but since they like the sun which tends to dry out the soil, you'll need to use mulch to preserve the soil's moisture. It is better to use black or brown mulch as this will help to retain moisture best as well as keeping the soil warm.

Cucumbers grow as bushes or vines and can be planted in containers, in rows, raised beds, or even vertically. Bush varieties grow well in containers while the vines will need a trellis which is easier to use in the garden.

Like the other vegetables in the cucumber family (the cucurbits), for example zucchini, pumpkins, and melons, they are heavy feeders and need to be supplemented well with nutrients. Work organic matter (compost, well-rotted manure) into the soil before to planting, and fertilizers will not be needed early on. But when they begin to blossom and fruit appears, add a balanced soluble fertilizer to help them produce their potential of thriving cucumbers in large number.

Cucumbers are ready for harvest in about 60 to 70 days after planting. Cucumbers need to be harvested when they are young and tender as they get bitter as they grow bigger. The slicing type cucumbers can be harvested when they are 6 to 8 inches long while pickling types are gathered at around 5 inches.

CARROTS

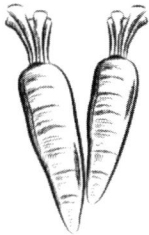

Carrots are usually grown from seed though you can buy punnets (small light basket) of seedlings. It is much more cost effective to sow seeds. Spread the seeds thinly so the carrots will not be crowded, and as seedlings emerge, remove any weak and spindly plants. Carrots require a lot of sun so choose a place that gets ample sunlight. The soil needs to be worked to a depth of at least twelve inches. Work in your soil amendment until it is mixed evenly but at the same time not overworked into a fine powder which can form a crust. Learn more about these popular root veggies.

HOW TO GROW PUMPKINS

Growing pumpkins is a lot like growing Zucchini's in that they are both low-to-the-ground growers with vines that can spread 4-6 inches a day. The yellow flowers that sprout out on these vines in about 40 days or so, develop into the gourd-like vegetable. The art of pumpkin growing can sometimes seem like a dark art to the uninitiated, but the fact is that it can be a lot of fun to learn how to grow them in a way that both maximizes their size and flavor.

The first decision that you need to make is whether you are growing the pumpkin to be used as a lantern at Halloween, or for eating in pumpkin pie. The reason is that different types of pumpkin are better for each use.

If you want a real monster pumpkin that you can carve out a face on and discard the innards, then you will generally be better off buying a Variety like a Howden.

CHAPTER 4: TIPS & TRICKS FOR THE BEST GARDEN

The practice of using raised beds for gardening is a wonderful and efficient method of gardening, but it can sure pose some challenges. Making some advanced planning for the issue that may arise in the future will ensure that the raised bed serves all the desired purposes.

Here are some factors that I usually put into consideration when planning to construct my raised bed garden. When these are put in place, they will help you get the most out of your gardening.

PRACTICAL CONSIDERATIONS

This will include making considerations about the height of the garden. The process of lifting materials such as watering cans used for watering the crops can be hard work if the raised bed is too high. Although for this there can be multiple solutions such as using irrigation systems, hoses or breakers. But lifting other heavier materials such as wheelbarrows loads of compost or heavy plants that are already in pots can be quite exhausting. To solve this, I suggest you create your raised bed with low ramps or scaffold board to push small amount of compost or soil up through a wheelbarrow.

WHEN HEIGHT BECOMES A PROBLEM

There are a variety of plants which grow up to be quite tall. Once they are planted on a raised bed, these tall climbing plants which include runner beans or hops actually end up being too tall for you to reach. They become so tall that you would have to make use of ladders to harvest or tie up the crops. To make it easier, it is better that you plant dwarf versions of these crops. These dwarf species are also as simple to grow as their taller versions and they make harvesting and maintenance quite easy.

CONSIDER BUDGETS

The cost of building and maintaining a raised bed garden is much higher than when growing crops directly into the soil. No matter the material that will be used for building the bed (bricks, rocks, lumber etc) they will have to be bought. Then there is also the cost acquired from planting the crops alone. While it is just easy to fill up home-made compost into the beds, the reality is that most raised bed are filled with materials imported into the garden. If money is spent to provide the initial outlay of the garden with quality, it will be worth it in the long term because the beds will last for longer and remain more efficient for other harvests.

Almost any material can be used to construct a raised bed as long as the material is strong enough to hold soil. It is best to avoid any material that can react with and contaminate the soil thereby affecting the soil and contaminating produce.

One example of such a contaminative agent is creosote that is found in old railroad ties. Asbestos is carcinogenic. What I look out for when searching for material is how available the material is, how attractive it would look and finally my personal taste. Here are some options you can go with

WOOD

Wood is cheap and easily available and it only requires basic skills to be able to construct a raised bed using wood. You should note the following while making a wood selection:

• Hard wood is generally more durable than softwood although softwood has been pressure treated and will most likely last longer.

• You can make use of gravel boards because of how light and strong they are. Plus additional boards can be added to create more depth each year if more compost is added to the bed.

• Railroad ties are known to give raised beds an attractive and rustic feel and provide a very sturdy structure. Because of their width, they provide a sitting area for the gardener after a mini stressful session of weeding and digging. But gardeners should be careful when making use of old recycled railroad ties as they capable of leaching out creosote and tar into the bed and contaminating the soil.

• Wooden pallets, logs or old scaffolds boards are also some very useful materials that can be used to construct raised beds.

• One major disadvantage of making use of wood while constructing a raised bed is that it will eventually rot and will need to be changed. Raised bed made of bricks and metals generally lasts longer.

BRICKS

Bricks are the ideal material to be used in producing a raised bed. I think they last the longest among all the other options. The thing with making use of bricks is that the gardener needs to have a certain level of bricklaying skill. The bed will require footings to prevent the walls from sinking. Any effort that is invested into the construction of the brick bed will be worth it because they are hard-wearing and the brick raised bed will last for years, sometimes almost as long as a brick house.

One major downside of using bricks is that you have to buy them and they are expensive to get, except if you have some old bricks that you can use. If not, then you can source for some second hand bricks on some community selling websites.

RECYCLED MATERIALS

There are plenty of recycled materials that can be used to construct a raised bed. Some of these can include rubber tires or old sandpits. Old roof tiles or bricks can be dug into the ground and filled up to form a low raised bed. Also, the chassis and framework of some scrap equipment like dilapidated cars can be used to build the raised bed.

TIPS ON PATHS FOR YOUR RAISED BED GARDEN

If you are to have multiple raised bed gardens, then you should consider having paths in between the gardens for easy movement. The paths are like the backbone of any garden and they add a sense of beauty and color to the whole aesthetic outlook. Functional paths will help you reach the key elements of your garden faster.

You should take a lot of consideration while choosing the final material with which the garden path will be constructed with. Most bricks raised beds mostly go with rustic woodchips path around it.

Creating paths using bricks or paving slabs

Paths that are been made with bricks or paving slabs are usually the sturdiest and they allow me to push my wheelbarrow around. You can dig them deep into the soil so that they become one with the ground. Put in some sand or some cement to fill in any leftover holes that may have been left unfiled. Then sprinkle in some water for it to become set.

You can find people who want to sell off their second hand bricks so that you get them at cheaper rates and you don't have to waste your money on brand new bricks.

Making use of grass

This one is a very cheap option, although I do not recommend it fully because of the amount of maintenance that has to be put into it to make it remain neat and fresh. The grasses have to be mowed at least once a week during the growing sessions. I use a shade-tolerant breed of grass to lay my paths so that they remain green all year long.

I have found out that for the path to stay as comfortable as ever, one has to make it as large as 20 inches wide. Remember that you will be pushing your wheelbarrow through those spaces and space will have to be large enough to be able to contain the equipment for easier movements. A path in which a wheelchair will be used should be as wide as 25 inches so that it will be easy to move through it.

Using gravel to lay the paths

I have come across some paths laid with gravels. Gravel paths are relatively cheap and very easy to construct. The only demerit of using gravel is that once you mistakenly drop soil or compost on it while working, it is quite hard to pack it up and discard.

Most gravel paths I have come across mostly make use of treated lumbers at the boundaries of the path to prevent the gravels from spilling to other sides. Use a roller or a wacker to compact down the ground and make it hold still.

To construct a herringbone brick path

Herringbone brick paths add a lot of overall beauty to the gardens. They give off this rustic effect when they are constructed between beds. I advise most people to go ahead with the method because they are quite easy to pull through during construction. Here is a simple step by step procedure that works out fine. To construct a herringbone brick path, you would need some sand and bricks.

• Dig out the soil where the path will be laid out. This is to ensure that the path is flush with the surface. Dig down as deep as 1 inch more than the height of the bricks that will be used.

• Fill in the path with sand up to a thickness of 1 inch.

• Then lay up the bricks in a herringbone pattern along the length of the path.

• Use a hammer to bed the bricks into the ground and brush in more sand into the gaps to fill up the gaps.

Creating a planting scheme that works for you will require a lot of planning. I spent a lot of time making all of my selections and choosing which plants I will be investing in. I advise that you first visualize how and what you want your garden to look like. Make adequate research on the plant requirements of the various plants you want to include.

The important question I ask myself is: What plant do I want to grow? The options open to me fall into any of these classes:

- Water Plants
- Alpines
- Herbs
- Grasses and Bamboos

- Vegetables
- Tress
- Bedding plants and annuals
- Shrubs

Fruit bushes

You can make use of a small piece of paper to put down whatever needs to be put down and regards the arrangement of the garden. After you may have selected what plants you will want to grow, then you should turn your considerations towards space.

For instance, whenever I decide on growing vegetables, I also plan out which vegetables will grow where. I plan out the spacing so that the growth of one plant will not affect the growth of another. Plus the planning is necessary so that you don't have taller plants shading lesser ones. I usually run crop rotation on my raised beds so that the nutrients in the soil are replenished from time to time.

If you want to go for ornamental crops, the plants that you chose must be suitable for the soil and the climatic condition in your area.

Color combinations

Whenever I decide to develop an ornamental bed consisting of ornamental crops, I think about the color combination of each plant. You should consider producing a raised bed with a single color theme so that it doesn't end up looking disorganized. Make a research on each of the plants and get creative while combining them. Consider the mood that each color combination will produce. I usually make use of a color wheel to balance out the colors and find the perfect match between them.

The color wheel has been a very useful help in selecting a color scheme for my ornamental crops. Look for art books and try to understand how the color wheel works. Most colors that are on the same side of the wheel mostly match and sit well with each other.

Considering size

In optimizing the arrangement of the raised bed, the various sizes of the plants should be considered. There is a rule I love to follow which is that I place the taller plants at the back and the shorter ones in front. It is like a progression, from the tallest to the smallest. The raised bed will, however, appear differently when it is viewed from various angles. I usually consider how I want my bed to be seen. If there are paths that travel around the various beds, then they will be seen from various angles so you won't have any problem.

A FEW REMINDERS

Have them face south

One of the best tips that one should never forget is to make sure that you lay out the beds horizontally so they can face the south of the garden. It will work best if the longest beds are the ones closest to the south.

The reason why this needs to be done is to make sure that all of the plants in the garden will receive the proper—and equal amount of lighting. However, by letting the end parts of the beds face the south, you are also limiting your chances of planting more crops, especially when variety is concerned. It will also limit sunlight from reaching small plants at the back. If you can remember, it is said that it's best to plant the tall plants at the back so that the small ones can get sunlight without any blockage.

A balanced diet

Plants need to have a great diet, too! Look for organic fertilizers and make sure that you use certain types of soil amendments that contain the following:

• Nitrogen, which is usually found in alfalfa meals, composted manure, and cover crops;

• Magnesium, which raises PH levels so plants won't dry up, and which can be found in Epsom salts;

• Calcium, just like people, plants also need calcium to grow strong. Calcium is usually found in lime or gypsum and provides nutrients most especially for acidic soil;

• Potassium, which can be found in greensand or kelp meal;

• Phosphorus, which can be found in rock phosphate and bone meal, and;

• Sulfur, but only if you're using Alkaline soil and if you need to lower PH levels of extremely acidic plants.

Providing your plants with these nutrients will make you breathe a sigh of relief as it's a sign that nutrient deficiency will be blocked.

Keep those pests away: Pests will do nothing good to your plants and one easy way to keep them away is by making sure that you lay galvanized mesh or hardware cloth across the bottom of the soil once it's on the bed already. Use ½ or ¼" layer of the said mesh cloth, and make sure that it continues up to 3" from where it was first laid on.

However, if you're trying to grow carrots, potatoes, and root crops, you have to remember to set the mesh as low as possible or just choose to buy raised garden planters in place of them. These would keep those crops safe.

Mulch between beds: Keep in mind that you should keep a perforated layer of landscape cloth on top of the soil when you are trying to weed out the pathways. Use 2 to 3" of coarse sawdust or bark mulch to cover this and let it reach up to 1" of the bottom of the bed. After that, you can then staple it to the bed so you won't have to mulch over and over again. Don't worry about esthetics because mulch will already be able to cover this.

Spread out the soil: By spreading out the soil, you can be sure that every plant you put in there will be able to receive equal amounts of nutrients, water, and sunlight. Of course, you can never be too sure about how equal it is, so you'd just have to add soil amendments, such as lime, compost, or peat and then top it off with topsoil. This way, they can all come together and eventually, you'll notice that they've all been spread out evenly!

Bed Leveling: It may be a bit meticulous to use bed levels but it will keep those beds safer, which in turn could lengthen their life. This way, you'll be able to use them more in years to come. What you have to do is put a 2 x 4" board on each side of the bed and tap the sides down until you reach the size that you desire.

Root Check: Don't forget to check for roots coming from other plants that may snatch the nutrients that are meant for the plants in your bed. When you see one, pull it out right away. Never allow the roots to grow. You can also install a root barrier.

And, never step on the soil!: Doing so would only make the soil compact, and as mentioned earlier, this isn't healthy for the plants. You can make use of a spanner board that you can place on the sides of the bed to prevent you from stepping in—you have no business there, anyway.

CHAPTER 5: IT IS SUITABLE FOR YOU

Companion planting works perfectly in raised beds. Those vegetables which need more space for their roots like carrots should be planted on top while others like leeks and onions will fill up space on the sides of your beds. The leeks and onions repel pests and will act as a shield for the carrot plants on the top of the bed.

These are but a few of the numerous benefits of gardening in raised beds. Therefore, it is not surprising to find that our modern-day gardeners are turning their attention with more frequency to this method. They have added a twist, though; now solid frames replace these sloping sides to give the raised beds a distinct and well-defined structure. What this means is that you can make the beds as high or tall as you want them to be without the danger of soil runoff when it rains.

It might sound like a huge job, but these modern raised gardening beds are easy to assemble or build by yourself. Frames can be built with concrete blocks, timber, or bricks and then filled with many organic materials mixed with soil. You will find kits ready for assembling as well as prefabricated plastic containers at almost any gardening center. Now anyone and everyone can easily and successfully grow their vegetables in raised beds and enjoy their own fresh produce.

BENEFITS OF RAISED BED GARDENING METHOD

Excellent Aeration

The older, traditional way to create raised beds is simply to dig up the soil, piling it into rows. You can follow this method and then support the two sides by using solid frames. Otherwise, place your frames in place and then fill them up with compost, farmyard manure mixed with quality soil. Whichever way you choose to do it, your plants will flourish in this enriched soil, and its loose structure will allow excellent air circulation around all the roots. We know that the different parts of plants all need to breathe, and so do the roots. For example, during photosynthesis, the leaves take in carbon dioxide and expel oxygen. If your plant sits in compact soil, the roots will suffocate and will not succeed in developing fully. This is because they need good aeration for their roots to be able to absorb the essential nutrients in the soil. To explain further, the soil bacteria convert the nitrogen in the little air pockets into nitrate salts and nitrate, thus providing the macronutrients for the plant. Without sufficient air, there is a lack of nitrogen, and therefore fewer nutrients will be available to the plant.

It is manifest that the population of microbes in your vegetable soil must be kept healthy, and this is made possible with well aerated soil. The balance of anaerobic and aerobic bacteria should be maintained as they all play their different roles to enhance the fertility of the soil.

Good Drainage

Even during a downpour of rain, your raised beds will render good drainage. No wonder this method is so popular in the tropics with its heavy rainfall. Because the soil has such a loose texture, water will seep slowly into the bed instead of making a quick runoff with the accompanying washing away of all fertile topsoil. Furthermore, all the excess water can easily drain away.

Although most plants do not mind moisture at all, they hate to get their feet wet. Firstly, all that water around their roots will make breathing almost impossible. Secondly, too much moisture will promote fungal and bacterial diseases. Lastly, excess water drenching the soil can change its pH level and raise the acidity. Plants that prefer more neutral or slightly alkaline soil will suffer as a result.

Some plants, for example, those that live in bogs, are adapted to grow in drenched soil, but most plants prefer soil with a twenty-five percent-moisture level. Raised beds will not allow water stagnation while at the same time, they keep your soil quite evenly moist because the water soaks into the lowest levels of your beds quickly.

The Spreading of Roots

Although plant roots can be quite persistent in their effort to grow, they will find it difficult to do so in tightly compacted soil. In loose soil they can grow and spread out to their hearts' content. Furthermore, a framed bed will retain the moisture after watering a lot longer than the more traditionally raised beds because the frames prevent water loss on the sides of the beds more effectively. Drying out of the beds can, therefore, be prevented and good root spreading will follow.

Plants growing in non-raised garden beds generally have a very shallow system of roots since they find it impossible to penetrate through the more compact soil deeper down unless of course, you go to the trouble of tilling the soil deeply before you plant your vegetables. This means that the plant roots are unable to get to the moisture kept in the deeper layers, which in turn may lead to dehydration of the plant when the moisture on the surface evaporates. Well-developed root systems anchor your plants. It also enlarges the potential food source area from which the plant can gather its nutrients and water. Vegetable plants, in particular, need enough of both to encourage vigorous growth and maximum yield during their relatively short growing season.

Minimum Risk of Compact Soil

A raised bed will not completely deter your smaller pets like dogs and cats from digging and rolling around in your gardening soil, but it definitely will keep humans and larger pets or animals at bay. This will prevent the tamping down of the soil. The ideal width for your raised beds is three to four feet, making it easy for you to do your gardening chores such as weeding, harvesting, and fertilizing without having to step onto the beds.

The floods, which sometimes occur after a heavy downpour, can also compact the soil of cultivated fields. Wet soil is heavy and will sink down and fill all the little air pockets. Once the water has evaporated, you will be left with a dense, hard layer that is not very accommodating for the plants. Raised beds allow the water to drain away much quicker, preventing floods to cause soil compaction.

Improved Weed Control

Sick and tired of weeding? A raised bed garden is the answer. In a normal vegetable plot, you will find it hard to get rid of all the frustrating weeds no matter how dedicated you are. They just seem to take over all the time.

When you cultivate the soil for normal vegetable beds, you expose a lot of the weed seeds that have been lying dormant underground shielded from the sun. The exposure to sunlight and extra moisture they receive during irrigation will provide them with the opportunity to start sprouting, just what they have been waiting for. Very quickly, they will feed on the nutrient-rich soil prepared for your vegetable plants and begin to flourish.

You can make use of the option to fill your raised beds with relatively weed-free soil and compost. If a few stray weeds appear, your raised beds with their loose soil will make weeding a breeze. A good tip is to fill up your raised beds with as many plants as will grow in them so that they will suffocate and outgrow any stubborn weeds that may try their luck.

Easier than Amending Existing Soil

Garden soil greatly varies from area to area; sometimes, it is more alkaline and chalky, often it is too acidic, and plants will not thrive without your intervention. Vegetables, in general, like slightly acidic to neutral soil, anything with a pH level of between 5.5 and 7.5. Having said that, there are exceptions. Blueberries and tomatoes, for instance, like more acidic soil while asparagus and broccoli prefer to have their roots in sweeter soil.

The remedy for alkaline soil is to add Sulphur, for acidic soil lime can be added. Sometimes applications have to be repeated several times to get the desired effect, but a downpour can undo all your hard work in a flash. It is not a simple, straightforward process to change the intrinsic nature of any type of soil.

If you plan to cultivate different kinds of vegetables, raised beds will give you the option of which soil you choose. On top of that, you can now fill up different raised beds with the type of soil each variety of vegetables prefers. The addition of lots of compost, something most gardeners usually do, makes it easier to sustain the soil's neutrality.

Garden on Top of Existing Turf

You have decided to start your vegetable garden, but the task of having to dig up and clean the existing turf presently growing in the area you have targeted is just too daunting. Do not despair; raised vegetable beds can be built straight on top of your grass without having to dig up any sods.

Mark your area, and then place multiple layers of cardboard and newspaper on the area. Erect your frames and then simply continue to fill them with grass clippings, soil, sand, decomposed farmyard manure, and compost. Plant your seeds or seedlings in this rich mixture, and you have started your garden without too much backbreaking labor.

Avoid Root Run from Larger Plants and Trees

Sometimes you will find that the only available space left in your garden for your vegetables is near several well-established trees. These trees have massively huge roots to anchor them to the ground and will devour all the nutrients in the soil, leaving very little for your vegetable plants. You may be able to get rid of some of these invasive roots, but it is an impossible task to get completely rid of them all. Using chemicals to try to kill the roots is not an option because these very same chemicals can harm or even kill your vegetable plants. However, your raised beds will be safe from this problem since tree roots generally grow downwards and will not reach into the raised beds.

More Effective Pest Control

Creepy crawlies are true to their description, they usually enter vegetable patches this way, crawling away until they find food. Encountering an obstacle like a solid frame will definitely deter some of them from crawling up. They may just pick the easier option of continuing along the ground. To protect your plants from soil parasites like nematodes, line your raised beds along the sides and the bottom with plastic. If you fear annoying rodents burrowing their way into your beds, use a netting of wire, placing it at the bases of your beds.

Overall, it will be easier to rid your beds of the various offenders just because they are more accessible. Applying chemical or natural pesticides or picking out invaders by hand is a lot less cumbersome if you do not have to bend down to ground level all the time. Everything, including nasty pests, will be more visible too. Walking along your raised beds, inspecting your plants regularly, you can quickly detect infestations and deal with them immediately. Remember, the sooner you tackle any pests, the easier it will be to rid your vegetable garden of them.

Extra Available Space

Raised beds in the traditional fashion provide more space for plants growing along the sides of the beds. Although this advantage does not apply to framed beds, they can provide additional space in another manner. Many of the plants growing along the side edges of the frames will extend over these side edges, leaving more room for other plants on the top surface of the bed. More light will be able to reach the plants as well.

Those varieties of tomatoes that normally will need staking can simply be allowed to grow downwards instead of upwards. Make sure the beds you plant them in are high enough. Strawberries and the vines of sweet potatoes tumbling down the sides of your raised beds will make a very pretty picture in your garden and create a luxurious aspect.

Extended Growing Season

We all know how long it takes the ground to thaw in spring, but raised beds speed up this thawing process. This means that you can start transplanting your seedlings much earlier in the season, giving them a wonderful head start. If the area where you live has a short window period to grow your edibles in the outside garden, this extra time will make a huge difference.

Some vegetables, for instance, onions, need a fairly long season to grow to maturity. Three to four months are needed for onion sets, and if you grow them from the seeds, it will take even longer. Seeds give you a much larger choice as only a few varieties are generally available assets. Making use of this advantage of choice means that you will need more time. Fortunately, onion seedlings like cooler weather, so plant them as soon as the soil in your raised beds has thawed.

Towards the end of the autumn, you can also extend your veggies' growing season; just place a few hoop covers onto your bed frames. This is easily done by installing pipe brackets made of metal from which you can attach or remove the hoop covers when necessary. Custom made covers in plastic or glass can be fitted for your individual raised beds as well.

Intensive Gardening with Higher Yield

It is a fact that a higher yield will be obtained by growing your veggies in raised beds rather than on flat ground beds. Attributing factors are the good aeration of the soil and extensive root run, but the main cause is the intensive nature of this kind of gardening. Raised beds allow you to plant a greater variety of different kinds of vegetables closer together than could be done on flat ground.

Because the soil used in these raised beds contains more organic matter and compost, it is rich enough to support quite several number of extra plants, definitely more than usual. The plants will fill up the beds as they continue to grow with their foliage touching. The close proximity of the plants will prevent weeds from flourishing too.

Solution for Mobility Challenged Gardeners

Not all gardeners are young, energetic, and healthy people. Many experienced gardeners find it difficult to continue bending down for weeding and tending their vegetable patches as they grow older and experience health challenges. Raised beds can be built or assembled to the exact width or height that will suit every individual. It can even be planned and laid out in a fashion to accommodate wheelchair users and allow them freedom of movement to plant and harvest their vegetables easily.

Even if you do not face any of these challenges, you will find it a relief to see those vegetable plants that need constant attention if they are raised off the ground. Backbreaking work is never fun and may even cause injuries. Salad vegetables and herbs need frequent harvesting, and popping out into the garden to pick a few herbs for your meal will be a lot easier if you do not have to bend down all the time.

Portability

If you find that your vegetable plants are not exposed to enough sunlight in their current spot, you can just move your raised bed without too much effort. Portability is one of the advantages of this method of gardening. Beds with wire bottoms can simply be dragged to a brighter location. Otherwise, dismantle the frames and then reassemble your beds in their new spots. With care, you can move the plants, as well as the soil, contend without any damage.

A very practical solution is to buy raised beds that are ready-made and fitted with casters. They are easily moved around, and if early frost overtakes you, they can even be rolled into your heated garage to save your plants.

There are quite several variations on the theme of raised bed gardening like the square foot, hay bale, and keyhole gardening. They all assist in making growing your own food less of a challenge and a lot more rewarding, something the modern age gardener appreciates.

CHAPTER 6: MOST COMMON MISTAKES

Many beginners gardeners plan to grow their vegetables in raised beds. If you are planning a raised bed garden for the first time this list will help you avoid many of the common mistakes of beginners.

1.   RAISED BED ARE TOO WIDE

One of the biggest benefits of raised bed gardening is avoiding soil compaction. You should be able to work in your garden bed withour stepping on them. This guarantees a better soil structure and finally healthier plants. For that reason raised beds should never be more than 4 feet wide. Most people can easily reach into the center of a four-foot-wide raised bed without any problem. Pls also consider the placement of the bed. If you situate your raised bed next to a fence, i recommend the width not to exceed thirty inches!

2.   YOU DO NOT PLAN FOR IRRIGATION

Unless you want to hand-water your raised beds you need to plan ahead of time how you will irrigate the beds. I would suggest placing the beds near a water source. Whether you plant to hand-water your beds or use a more efficient system of soaker hoses or drip lines, having water easily accessible will save you much time and headache.

I recommend soaker hoses or drip irrigation for raised beds. For just a few raised beds, soaker hoses will perform just fine. Instead if you have many beds or if you garden with a combination of raised beds and ground beds, setting up a drip irrigation system works great and costs less.

3.   UNSAFE MATERIAL

Do not use pressure-treated wood manufactured prior to 2003. Actually this contains chromated copper arsenate, and you don't want that near your food garden! Modern methods of pressure-treated wood use safer practices and it is your choice to use them. Some people choose to use rot-resistant and chemical -free woods such as cedar or redwood, but prepare to pay more if you got that route.

4.　　　RAISED BED GARDEN SOIL LACKS NUTRIENTS

Many soil combinations will work well with raised beds, but some do not. Potting soil, for example, drains too quickly. Unless your raised bed sits on concrete or rocks (and thus acts more like a container), skid the potting soil. You need more substance than what potting soil can provide.

Another usual mistake is using soil with too much nitrogen content, like a bed full of composted manure or a bag of soil filled with chemical fertilizers- your plants will grow great but fruit-producing plants like tomatoes produce little fruit. I also have found that plants grown in a raised bed filled only with bagged soil grew much slower than those beds with some amount of organic material mixed in.

Personally I got the best success using a combination of native soil (or garden soil) and organic material like compost, but depending on what you have available and your budget, there are many options to choose from.

5.　　　RAISED BEDS ARE PLACED TOO CLOSE TOGETHER

Working in raised beds can be the joy of any gardener. That's why you should create the most comfortable working area as possible.

To do this remember to put enough room between the beds – two to three feet at least. Otherwise it will be a challenge weeding, planting, and harvesting from those edges.When you place your raised beds, ensure you can get your garden cart or wheelbarrow in between them. When you have enough space to do that, you can sit a stool beside the beds for a comfortable working area.

6.　　　PATHWAYS GROW UP WITH WEEDS AND GRASS

There are few things more frustrating than going out to my garden, planning to enjoy some time working in my raised beds, and discovering the grass has grown up beside them. If you don't want to keep mowing or weed eating the grass and weeds around your beds, place a barrier down before the weeds and grass emerge for the season.

Broken down cardboard boxes with a light layer of mulch on top works great! I do recommend organic mulches. Skip the landscape fabric because weeds will eventually get through anyway. Pine needles are my favorite for pathways because they break down more slowly than other materials.

7.   NEGLECTING TO MULCH RAISED BEDS

Mulching your raised beds is just an important as mulching in a ground garden bed, and perhaps even more so.

Though weed pressure is usually less in raised beds, it isn't non-existent. Weed seeds from native soil find light and sprout. Seeds floating in the wind and deposited from birds love the rich soil of raised beds. For these reasons, mulch will dramatically reduce your weeding time.

But more importantly, mulch regulates the soil temperature and retains moisture – both critical needs of raised beds in the hot summer.

One huge advantage of raised beds is how the soil heats up quicker in the spring, allowing for faster planting. But it also heats up as the season goes on. Mulch helps regulate that temperature more than bare soil would.

Mulch also regulates moisture. In wet seasons, it acts like a sponge, absorbing excess rainfall. In dry times, it keeps moisture from evaporating in the heat of the summer. You will find your mulched raised beds much healthier than those without it.

Hopefully, by avoiding these 7 mistakes , you will be on your way to an enjoyable raised bed gardening experiences with abundant harvest!

CONCLUSION

Thank you for making it to the end of **Raised Bed Gardening** starting a raised bed garden is a great way to accommodate that budding little gardener in your family. It is the ideal way for kids to learn about nature; they will see the wonder of a little seedling emerging from the ground, growing tiny leaves and later develop into a mature plant with fruit. Planting in raised beds will make it convenient for both you and the young ones to reach every plant in the box without ending up with muddy feet or knees full of dirt.

Now that you have all the information needed, it is time to get going. Walk around your available space during the day to find a sunny location. Once you have decided where you want to place your raised bed, decide on the size and dimensions. The next step is to make a list of everything you will need, from the soil, compost and other materials, to the frames. Once your bed is up and filled up with the soil mixture, it is time to turn your attention to the plants. Select the type of veggies you want to grow according to the guidelines I have provided. If you want to grow plants from seeds, you will have to do some prior planning since it will take time for them to develop into seedlings ready to be planted outside in your box. Otherwise, you can purchase seedlings to plant directly into your raised beds.

A well planned garden alongside the selection of the right soil is the secret to successful raised bed gardening. These gardening tactics are not new inventions; in fact, they have been practiced in some form or the other from ages. Raised bed gardens are becoming increasingly popular in the US today. Certain technical aspects of the planning may vary from region to region, but the fundamentals are the same virtually everywhere. If applied skillfully, these techniques can result in a far better production rate (as much as 4 to 10 times better according to some estimates) than what you would achieve through orthodox gardening methods in an average fertile land.

One of the most important factors that make raised beds so effective and efficient is that the crops get the chance to grow in just the right type of soil - deep, fertile and loose enough to yield higher production rate. This is possible because the overall condition throughout the setup is favorable towards proper soil drainage as well as aeration, which in turn enables plant-roots to penetrate deeper.

Apart from that, maintenance is also easy in any raised bed garden. Removing weeds and rubbles hardly takes any time, enabling you to focus more on other important tasks such as watering the plants. Since the gardener will always be standing in the pathway, the plants never have to face the risk of being stepped on. Unlike the traditional gardening tactics, you can concentrate your soil amendment and improvisation efforts on the beds only, not on the pathway. This, needless to say, helps you save on both resources and time.

The appeal of raised bed gardening is that it hardly requires any special care or attention. The only factors that you will ever have to worry about are watering the plants, planting and harvesting them at the proper time and periodically removing minimal amounts of weed from the garden. Whenever you harvest a plant, add some compost into the empty space and then replant.

The type of the soil as well as the wall material used for constructing the raised beds play a pivotal role in the overall health of the plants and your garden. Proper spacing between the plants is also crucial - if congested, they won't get enough room to grow freely. On the other hand, if there's just too much space in between them, your production rate will suffer, and weeds are encouraged to grow. You also must be careful to choose plants that will grow favorably in your climate.

The next step for you is to take a walk around your potential raised bed garden area and do some planning. Remember, if you have good sun, good soil, and plenty of water you're going to be okay. Good luck and happy harvesting!

PART II

COMPANION PLANTING

INTRODUCTION

Surely by now, you have gained interest in companion planting, but at the same time, you may be in doubt as to whether or not this thing really works. Well, here are some facts that will likely convince you that companion planting is no joke and that several individuals have actually experienced the marvelous results.

Companion planting promotes the maximum growth and development of the plants placed side by side in a plot. One way it works is based on the amount of shading that is necessary for the promotion of optimal growth. Some plants may require minimal shade while others seem to grow best when not exposed to too much sunlight. Being the case, one plant could actually provide the shade that the other plant needs so that both benefit from this setup.

Some plants produce chemicals or substances and efficiently export them out of the system without harming themselves or the plants surrounding them. What is beneficial about these substances is that they actually promote the growth of neighboring plants as the chemicals appear to act as signals or sensors, which promote the production of substances in the other plant. The substances appear to be advantageous to the plant as they encourage food production or cell propagation.

Some substances produced by the plants also seemed to have a negative impact on many pests. The substances appear to be detrimental or irritating to the animals and so they do not actually land and feed on the plants. A typical example would be onions. When planted together with another plant, onions produce substances that drive pests away. Still, others have secretions that tend to redirect the pests or insects away from the more desirable plants to plants that are less palatable to them.

The sweet-smelling flower, when planted beside a plant that is typically monochrome, attracts pollinators that can potentially pollinate both plants. As a result, you get your plants propagated faster and enhance genetic quality as self-pollination is less likely to happen.

ADVANTAGES OF COMPANION PLANTING

Companion planting is pretty much a bandwagon these days. In fact, you might find that your neighbors are already creating their own version of a companion garden.

So what's the deal with this form of planting and why should you be enticed to join those who are currently practicing this? You can actually look at these advantages from two angles: what you can directly obtain and what you can contribute to the sustenance and perhaps the preservation of the environment.

DIRECT BENEFITS

You plant because you perhaps intend to have a fresh source of veggies, herbs, and cut flowers without leaving your home. One of the direct benefits is you can actually harvest healthier and better quality crops. This is because the plants actually help each other to grow not just vigorously but also to reach their best potential.

The crops produced from companion planting are also better not just in appearance but in taste. You enjoy more the products of your home garden and so you can savor more great recipes, which you can enjoy alone or with the company of your family members and friends.

The old adage "Catching two birds with one stone" actually applies when you practice companion planting. This is because the plants that you beside each other need not be all veggies or all flowers. In fact, the most popular combinations are those of vegetables and a flower or herbs and a flower. Therefore, you need not have several plots for a single plot; for instance you may actually have a source of fresh cuts of flowers and healthy veggie choices.

Your home plots will never look as ordinary as before. The mixture of different plants improves the appearance of your garden plots. Unlike the typical monotonous look, your garden will have an eye-catching and enticing transformation. This is possible because you tend to do strip planting, where one strip will be filled with flowers and the parallel strip is planted with a green, leafy veggie.

Companion planting does not require a large patch of land. Even if you have just a small area on your lawn that you can allot for planting, you will harvest a variety of fresh crops. In this way, you do not leave a portion of your lawn idle but instead, maximize what you can actually do with just a small space.

CHAPTER 1: WHAT'S COMPANION PLANTING?

Some individuals may consider companion planting to be some kind of 'New Age' holistic fad; however, as the good book says 'There is nothing new under the sun.'

Although the whole aspect of companion planting seems finally to have gathered some recognition; the fact is that it has been practiced for centuries – ever since man first picked up a shovel and decided to grow his own food rather than (or as well as), chase it around with a bow and arrow!

Infact, companion planting could be seen as the very foundation stone upon which the whole organic or green movement is built; the reason for this is simple. If done properly, companion planting does away with the need for chemical fertilizers and bug sprays; produces the best, healthy crops; and is the most environmentally friendly way to produce your own fresh food consequently.

Not only can you save money by 'going green,' but by making use of the companion planting methods described in this book, you – and your children – can live healthier lives by cutting out the chemical fertilizers and pesticides, that are inevitably included in the daily diet of those individuals who couldn't care less about what they consume, or indeed how it has been grown.

Companion planting is simply a form of polyculture, and when used intelligently along with gardening techniques such as Raised Bed Gardening, Square Foot Gardening, or Container Gardening for instance; then this method of sharing the mutual benefits of the individual plants, can produce fantastic results.

In fact, companion planting is likened to putting together the perfect partnership; creating results in respect of larger, healthier crops that the individual plants could not produce.

The fact is that, just like we homo-sapiens, plants need good companions to thrive and flourish in their environment. Unlike us however, being rooted to the spot, they cannot choose their friends – we must choose friends or companions for them!

How do we choose 'friends' that they will like, and get along with? Simple really. We take into account the strong points and needs of the individual plants, and then put them together – in fact the gardener takes on the role of match-maker!

The fact is that if the plants thrive – alongside the ideal companions that you have provided - then the harvest is bountiful – and everyone is happy.

Companion planting is the planting of different plants in close proximity that will provide different benefits for each other. Some plants will thrive when grown together as they will not be competing for light, other plants will thrive together because one plant will attract beneficial insects and the other plant will provide shelter. It is a beneficial relationship between different plants.

Using companion planting to its maximum not only increases the likelihood of thriving plants but it also gives you an opportunity to make better use of your available space. Creating this diversity creates an environment that is more like growing conditions found in the wild.

Our obsession with planting large groupings of similar plants, often referred to as monoculture has exposed our food crops to a greatly increased risk of attack from disease and insects. Crop rotation can help to reduce the risk, but crop rotation alone is not enough.

HISTORY OF COMPANION PLANTING

The history of companion planting is not particularly known as it isn't very well documented. There are stories and oral traditions from cultures all over the world, but the origins are not clear. The three sisters' method of growing corn, squash, and beans is thought to date back thousands of years to when humans first inhabited the Americas. In China, mosquito ferns have been planted with rice crops to fix nitrogen for at least a thousand years. As the organic culture became more popular in the late 1960's and 1970's, so companion planting also grew in popularity as a natural method of gardening. For many home gardeners, reducing the requirement for chemicals can only be a good thing, and it benefits the environment and wildlife too.

Companion planting is considered a traditional practice when growing fruit and vegetables on a smaller scale, typically used by the backyard gardener or allotmenteer. In the last thirty to forty years though, it has developed as a practice used in larger scale operations, which includes intercropping. With a strong focus from the scientific community on improving food production while promoting sustainable farming practices, companion planting is gaining ground as scientists conclude what we've been saying for years … it works!

CHAPTER 2: BENEFIT OF COMPANION PLANTING

Companion planting is receiving a lot of attention from the scientific community because it can help reduce the need for harmful chemicals in farming. Home gardeners are re-discovering this information and using it to their benefit.

There are several different ways in which companion planting can help you, including:

• Pest Repellent – certain plants give off chemicals either from their leaves, flowers, or roots which will repel or suppress pests, protecting their neighbors. Some pests spread diseases, but keeping the bugs under control will help prevent those diseases from taking over your plot. A lot of gardeners will use chemicals to control pests, so this natural pest control is more in line with organic gardening methods and helps reduce your need for chemical sprays. Catnip, for example, can repel aphids, ants, and weevils, but also keeps mice away, but not just because it attracts cats. It can take as long as a year or two for natural chemicals to build up in the soil to provide this defense, as is the case with marigolds, which deter nematodes. Some people will claim that companion planting doesn't work purely because they've not given the plants enough time to work their magic.

• Nitrogen Fixers – beans, clover, peas and some other plants have nodules on the roots which grow Rhizobium bacteria. These helpful bacteria take nitrogen from the atmosphere and fix it into the soil in a form that can be used by plants. This nitrogen fixing also benefits neighboring plants as well as later crops planted in the same location.

• Sacrificial Planting – if you have a plant that is particularly susceptible to a pest, you plant another plant nearby that the pests prefer as a decoy. The pests flock to that plant, rather than your vegetable crop. You will still get some pests on your vegetables, but not as many. Most of them will be on the sacrificial plant and can then be easily disposed of. Collard greens planted near cabbage keep the diamondback moth away as they are more attracted to the greens. Mustard is another trap crop as it attracts cabbage worms (caterpillars) and harlequin bugs, which are extremely destructive to everything from cabbages to radishes for beetroot and potatoes, to mention just a few. Don't pull the mustard up to dispose of the harlequin bugs because they will fall off and make their way to other plants. Dunk the stems (by bending them) into soapy water, so the bugs drown. Plant mustard with clover or dill to attract parasitic wasps, which will prey on the harlequin bugs.

• Enhancing Flavor – some pairings will improve the flavor of your vegetable crop. One of the best-known examples of this is the pairing of basil and tomatoes. These work fantastically in the kitchen, but when grown together, the basil makes the tomatoes more flavorsome. Many herbs, when grown with vegetables, improve their flavor. German chamomile (wild chamomile) improves the flavor and growth of onions, cabbages, and cucumbers.

• Camouflage - a lot of pests use smell to find your precious crops, or they look for the shape of your plant. By choosing companion plants with a strong smell, you can confuse many pests. For those pests that hunt by sight, companion plants can confuse the shape of the plant too.

• Shading – known as stacking in permaculture or as level interactions, is the principle of planting taller plants so that they provide shelter and shade for more delicate plants. This relies on you knowing the path of the sun through the sky. One example of this is the three sisters method of planting where the corn provides welcome shade for the squash plants.

• Attracting Beneficial Insects – your garden needs pollinators as well as pest predators such as hoverflies, lacewings, spiders, parasitic wasps, predatory mites, and ladybirds. Planting the right companion plants will attract insects, which will keep the problem pests down and pollinate your vegetable plants. Creating the right environment for these beneficial insects will encourage them to spend their entire life-cycle in your vegetable garden. This is more important than you may think because it is the larvae of many insects that devour problem pests.

• Increasing Biodiversity – a good mix of plants creates a much more resilient ecosystem. Pests, adverse weather conditions, and diseases will not wipe out your entire crop, but instead just damage a portion of it, and even that can be minimized with the right planting. Companion planting has a lot of benefits, and it is something that many more gardeners can benefit from. In this book, you will learn how you can use companion planting in your vegetable garden and increase your yields while decreasing your work. It doesn't take up extra space and doesn't detract from your main crops. It means your plants are healthier, grow better, and can taste much nicer.

CHAPTER 3: COMPANION PLANTING STRATEGIES

For people with limited space, a garden that uses companion planting is the perfect solution to growing vegetable plants and increase their harvest.

To make this practice work, however it is necessary to do some planning ahead of time on your part to optimize the yield when harvest time rolls around.

But some tips will increase the output of your crops during this season. They have been found to work very well with the companion planting method and are mutually beneficial to both plant types.

There are many different benefits to this practice and some of the more popular ones include increasing the size and number of products that is made, repelling garden pests that may otherwise wreak havoc on your plants, and attract beneficial predators that can eat the invaders and keep your plot safe.

Just because you have limited space doesn't mean that you can't enjoy a bumper crop of vegetables. By putting some of the following methods to use, you will see some marvelous results in the fall.

One such way is through interplanting. This is slightly different from companion planting because it makes the most use of a small plot and the plants typically have more than one purpose. A perfect example of this method is using squash and corn in the same area along with bean plants. The corn stalks tend to grow tall and act as a support for the bean vines, while the squash produces large leaves that not only shield the ground to deter weed growth but also act as a natural barrier to corn pests.

Vegetables and flowers can also be interplanted for good results. This is actually one of the best ways to attract pollinators and natural predators to garden pests.

Succession planting is another popular method of putting in a garden plot and this has been used to extend the growing season.

There are 4 ways that succession planting can be implemented. The first involves planting the same species but putting plants in at different time intervals. The second entails planting different vegetables in successive periods. You can also plant 2 vegetables in the same area in the third method, while the fourth way is planting the same vegetable but using ones that mature at different rates.

A final option is putting in plants that are annuals (i.e. they only need to be put in once) in order to enjoy multiple yields from one planting. These include such things as asparagus, rhubarb, and sweet potatoes just to name a few of the more popular varieties. With the proper soil preparation, you can plant any number of varieties and enjoy a bountiful harvest for many years.

GROW YOUR COMPANION HERB GARDEN

The best thing about growing an herb garden is the ease of maintenance. Most of them don't need daily watering or fertilization. But you still need to weed!

Most veteran gardeners use a technique called deep watering which means irrigating the area until there are small puddles evident.

Pest issues are another story altogether. Since you will want to eat these plants at some point, an organic method is preferred to treat them. It's not hard so don't fret about making your solution. In a one-quart handheld sprayer, add a squirt of ivory soap or baby shampoo, then fill with warm water.

NEVER use detergent in this manner. This is just the basic formulas as it can be added to as necessary when combating a specific pest. You should always test the mixture in a small area before proceeding to make sure that the plants are resistant.

If you want to make sure it sticks well to the plants, add 1 teaspoon of vegetable oil. You can also take 1/2 cup of mineral oil and add crushed garlic cloves to it. Strain this mixture after letting it stand for 48 hours. Add about 1 teaspoon to the water/soap mixture. Another alternative uses one bulb of garlic and onion. Puree this in a blender/food processor. Put into one cup of olive oil and let sit for 48 hours. Strain the mixture and throw out the pulp. Now add 1/2 teaspoon of cayenne pepper and store in a glass jar. You can add 1 teaspoon to the soap spray as needed.

If you would rather not use any type of spray in your plot, there is always companion gardening. This means planting herbs next to the plant to keep bugs away. Just find a plant that has a natural predatory insect such as aphids and plant an herb next to it to keep them at bay. This is just one good example of using herbs in order to combat these types of insects naturally, so you may want to do further research on specific companion types. However, using herb plants as a natural means of keeping out invaders is a great way to still enjoy your garden time and avoid the use of unnecessary chemicals that not only enter the water supply but become a part of the food chain as well.

CHAPTER 4: TYPES OF INSECTS

GOOD INSECTS

There are literally millions of types of insects, but not all of them are pests determined to devour your crops. There are a lot of species that are referred to under the umbrella term of 'beneficial insects' which provide a natural form of pest control. Many gardeners, including myself, are an essential part of organic and natural gardening.

Here are some of the most commonly found beneficial insects with information about what they eat and the environment they prefer.

Ladybugs

These carnivorous insects feed on green and black aphids as well as red spider mites. Organic growers and gardeners love them, trying to attract these into their gardens. Every year ladybugs, or ladybirds as they are known in the UK, will lay hundreds of eggs. The larvae will eat thousands of aphids before maturing, hence the importance of providing a habitat for both this insect in both adult and larvae form. Typically, a ladybug will live for up to three years so long as it avoids being another predator's lunch!

Several plants attract ladybugs, including:

- Tansy
- Fennel
- Dill
- Cinquefoil

- Yarrow
- Alyssum
- Penstemon

Ladybugs feed on some common garden pests, including:

- Aphids
- Colorado potato beetles
- Fleas

- Mites
- Whitefly

Spiders

A surprising number of people don't like spiders, which is understandable as they aren't my favorite critter either. However, they are very useful in the garden as they eat a lot of different pests. Spiders will naturally find a home in your garden, but you can attract more to your vegetable plot.

Ground Beetles

These are your best friend as they are very voracious predators. These will eat almost anything but are particularly fond of slugs and snails! Their eating habits will mean they won't get invited to the dinner table; they vomit on their prey, and the digestive enzymes start to dissolve their food.

Ground beetles are often killed by beer traps put down for slugs, as they walk along and fall in. Make sure there is a lip on your beer trap that will prevent these beneficial predators from drowning in the beer.

Most ground beetles are nocturnal and need somewhere shady to hide during the day. A pile of stones or logs or some leaf litter will give them a good place to hide out during the day.

Ground beetles are attracted to your garden by several plants, including:

- Clover
- Amaranthus
- Evening Primrose

The ground beetle will dine on many different pests, including:

- Slugs and snails

- Cutworms
- Colorado potato beetles
- Caterpillars

These are worth protecting and looking after in your garden because they will help to keep the pest levels down naturally.

Parasitic (Braconid) Wasps

These are very different from the wasps that bother a lot of gardeners. They tend to be smaller and will not sting you, unlike their bigger and more vicious cousins.

The lifecycle of these wasps is considered a little gruesome, but they benefit your garden in helping to control pest levels. This wasp will lay its egg in host insects. Once the egg has hatched, the larvae eat the host alive and then emerge as an adult. This family of wasps hunts many different pests including caterpillars, ants, aphids, and sawflies.

A wide variety of plants attracts parasitic wasps, including:

- Yarrow
- Dill
- Parsley
- Lemon Balm
- Lobelia
- Marigold
- Cosmos
- Alyssum
- Cinquefoil

They prey on a lot of different destructive insects, including:

- Aphids
- Caterpillars
- Tomato hornworm
- Tobacco hornworm

Damsel Bugs

Another great insect to attract into your garden, these are not fussy eaters and will prey on pretty much any insect that causes problems in your garden. In Europe, they live in orchards where they eat gypsy moths and red spider mites. This insect will overwinter in vegetation and appreciates somewhere to hide out between meals.

Damsel bugs are attracted to your garden by plants including:

- Alfalfa,
- Fennel
- Caraway
- Spearmint

They eat lots of common garden pests, including:

- Aphids
- Cabbage worms
- Caterpillars
- Corn earworms

- Leafhoppers
- Potato beetles
- Spider mites

By growing some ground cover and low hanging plants, you can attract damsel bugs into your garden where they can help control pests.

Green Lacewings

These are particularly attractive insects that are common in British gardens. With their delicate, lacy wings you could be forgiven for thinking these innocent little creatures are of no use in your garden.

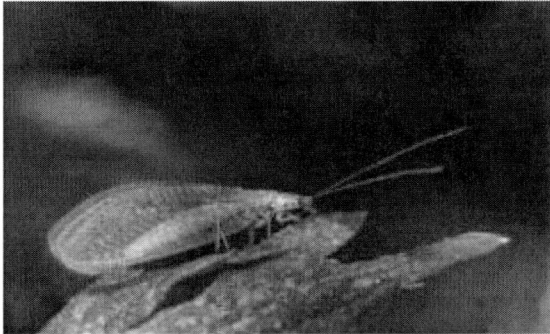

Don't be fooled by their good looks! These are voracious predators in both adult and larvae forms and will eat vast amounts of insect eggs and aphids. The larvae have large jaws which interlock to make pincers on which their prey is impaled. The larvae are very good at clearing your garden of soft-bodied pests.

Lacewings are attracted into your garden by several different plants, including:

- Angelica
- Coriander
- Cosmos
- Dandelion
- Dill
- Fennel
- Yarrow

Some of the insects eaten by lacewings include:

- Aphids
- Caterpillars
- Leafhoppers
- Mealybugs
- Whitefly

Soldier Beetles

Both adults and larvae are useful in pest control. The female lays her eggs in the soil where they overwinter, pupating in the spring. Therefore, you need to leave some areas of soil undisturbed to overwinter so these eggs can mature.

Soldier beetles also eat pollen, so pollen-bearing plants can help to attract them into your garden. Other plants that attract them include:

- Goldenrod
- Marigold
- Milkweed
- Wild lettuce
- Zinnia

These beneficial insects prey on many different insects, including:

- Aphids
- Caterpillars
- Corn rootworms
- Cucumber beetles
- Grasshopper eggs

These are interesting insects to look at and will help keep pests under control.

Tachinid Flies

Adult tachinid flies closely resemble the typical housefly and so are often mistaken for them. These are parasitic insects and lay their eggs in host insects. Depending on the species of fly, either eggs or live young are placed inside a host insect where they then eat their way out. Some species will even lay eggs on plants where host insects live which then hatch and eat them.

Tachinid flies can be bought, or you can attract them into your garden with a variety of plants including:

- Aster
- Buckwheat
- Carrots
- Cilantro (coriander)
- Chamomile
- Dill
- Fennel
- Feverfew
- Parsley
- Ox-eye and Shasta daisies

They prey on a lot of different pests, including:

- Caterpillars
- Colorado potato beetles
- Corn earworms
- Cutworms
- Earwigs
- Gypsy moths
- Japanese beetles
- Mexican bean beetles
- Sawfly beetles
- Squash bugs

Hoverflies

These are frequently confused with wasps as they share a black and yellow coloring, but they do not sting. They also hover (which wasps do not), do not have long antennae, and are typically smaller than stinging wasps. There are lots of different species of hoverflies, and they can fly as fast as 40km/h in short bursts.

Hoverflies will naturally find their way into your garden, but you can attract more of them with plants such as:

- Alyssum
- Cosmos
- Dill
- Lemon balm

- Mallow
- Marigold
- Yarrow

Hoverfly larvae prey on some garden pests including:

- Aphids
- Caterpillars
- Scale insects

Predatory Mites

Humid environments attract these mites such as polytunnels (hoop houses) and greenhouses, where they are most welcome as they prey on spider mites! Spider mites can be a serious problem in greenhouses and very hard to control.

Predatory mites can find their way into your greenhouse, but more often people will buy these beneficial insects and introduce them to the environment.

When there are no spider mites for them to feed on, they will feed on pollen from your plants, helping with pollination.

Solitary Bees

There are lots of species of solitary bee, which does not live in colonies, choosing to live by themselves instead. In Britain alone, there are over 200 different species of solitary bee, including the masonry bee, which is often mistaken for a hornet or wasp.

These bees can look like wasps or honeybees, but they are no threat whatsoever to you. The females dig nests, which are then stocked with food (nectar and pollen) and sealed. The young are left to fend for themselves. These bees will usually nest under the ground, often being found under sheds, in piles of logs, and so on. You can help encourage them to your garden by making an insect hotel.

These are vital pollinators and should be encouraged into your garden with flowering plants such as:

- Catnip
- Fuchsia
- Heather
- Lavender
- Marjoram
- Viburnum

You now know about some of the beneficial insects that you want to attract into your garden. Of course, there are many more insects, and some will depend on where in the world you live. In some areas praying mantis is a beneficial insect, but here in England, I won't ever see one in the wild.

Growing the right types of plants will help attract these insects into your garden and should be part of any gardener's plan. Chemicals should be avoided where possible because they indiscriminately kill both beneficial and harmful insects. With certain chemicals, the residue will persist for the rest of the growing season, which can prevent beneficial insects from returning.

BAD INSECTS

While the perfect garden would only attract beneficial insects that would prey on anything and everything that dared step foot into the garden, that's rarely the case. Most gardens contain a wide variety of insects, both good and bad.

Let's take a closer look at some of the more common pests found in gardens across the country. If you're lucky, you won't have to deal with more than one or two of these insects at once.

Aphids

Aphids, also known as plant lice, are tiny little insects that can quickly multiply into a huge problem that spans across the vast majority of a garden. A single aphid making its way into an unprotected garden can result in millions or even billions of aphids quickly populating every nook, cranny and corner of your garden.

Aphids can have up to 12 live babies per day. Within the first week, one aphid can have 84 babies. Within a week those aphids are ready to start having babies of their own. The 84 babies will start adding 12 babies apiece per day, which is more than 1,000 aphids being added daily. Once they start having babies, the numbers jump even more dramatically. Within a month, millions of aphids will be infesting the garden. Of course, this simple scenario assumes no aphids die and that each of the aphids has exactly 12 babies per day, but you get the point.

Luckily, you have some options when it comes to control aphids. You can plant caraway, chamomile, dandelions, buckwheat and tansy to attract insects that prey on them. Ladybugs, green lacewings, praying mantises and minute pirate bugs will all make a meal of aphids. Nasturtiums can be used as a trap crop for aphids.

Additionally, you can use the following plants to repel aphids

- Basil.
- Catnip.
- Chives.
- Clover.
- Coriander.
- Dill.
- Eucalyptus.
- Fennel.
- Garlic.
- Onions.
- Nettles.
- Peppermint.
- Radishes.

A combination of plants that attract insects that attack aphids and plants that aphids don't care for seems to be the best way to prevent aphids from making their way into the garden. If you catch an infestation while it's underway, use a strong spray of water to wash aphids away from your plants. Watch your plants closely after that and wash them down again if the aphids return.

Asparagus Beetles

Asparagus beetles are orange and white or blue-black beetles that prey on asparagus shoots. From larvae to mature adults, asparagus beetles will make a meal of both the leaves and the stems of the asparagus plant. Knock the larger beetles into a bucket of soap to get rid of them.

Ladybug larvae will eat both the eggs and the larvae of the asparagus beetle, so keep plants that attract ladybugs in your garden. Additionally, the following plants are known to deter asparagus beetles:

- Basil.
- Petunias.
- Coriander.
- Tomatoes.
- Parsley.

Cabbage worms and Cabbage Loopers

Cabbage worms and cabbage loopers attack Brassica crops all across North America. They look like white or green caterpillars and will tunnel through the roots of cabbages.

Beneficial nematodes are the main predator needed in the garden to clear out cabbage worms. Nematodes will likely have to be purchased because they are difficult to attract. In addition to adding nematodes to the soil, the following plants can be grown to prevent cabbage worms from ever making their way into a garden:

- Borage.
- Rosemary.
- Celery.
- Sage.
- Dill.
- Thyme.
- Radishes.
- Tomatoes.

Another option is to plant a crop like mustard that attracts cabbage loopers and cabbage worms around the outside of your garden as a trap crop that can be sacrificed to protect more desirable crops.

Caterpillars

Caterpillars attack a wide range of plants, chewing on leaves, tunneling through fruit and leaving droppings behind everywhere they go. While the butterflies some of them will eventually become may be beneficial to a garden, they are quite the pest while in the caterpillar stage. Of particular concern are cutworms and cabbage loopers, which have been known to quickly strip plants of their foliage.

To keep caterpillars at bay, add plants to your garden that draw in parasitic wasps, praying mantises, and green lacewings. Another option is to hang a bird feeder to call in birds that'll come for the bird food and supplement their meals with any caterpillars that cross their paths. When you see a caterpillar, handpick it and move it far from your garden.

The following plants can be planted in a garden to repel caterpillars:

- Lavender.
- Peppermint.
- Sage.

Colorado potato beetle

The Colorado potato beetle looks like a yellowish-orange ladybug with stripes instead of dots. While ladybugs are a preferred predator in the garden and will eat Colorado potato beetles, these pests will quickly defoliate peppers, potatoes, eggplant and tomatoes. In addition to ladybugs, nematodes are beneficial to have around when potato beetles are present.

Some sources indicate the Colorado potato beetle doesn't like to walk over coarse mulch. Adding a layer of straw mulch around your plants may prevent the beetle from making it to your plants.

The following plants will repel Colorado potato beetles:

- Catnip.
- Chives.
- Coriander.
- Eucalyptus.
- Garlic.
- Green beans.
- Marigolds.
- Nasturtiums.
- Peas.

Flea Beetles

These tiny little pests are found across the entirety of North America. They chew small, round holes in the leaves of most vegetables and will jump around nervously when disturbed. Flea beetles prefer dry soil to lay their eggs in, so keep your soil damp to make your garden less attractive. Nematodes can be added to the soil to make short work of any larvae that do hatch.

The following plants will repel flea beetles:

- Catnip.
- Peppermint.
- Rue.
- Thyme.

Mealybugs

Mealybugs are tiny creatures that appear in clusters at the base of leaves. They'll attack a wide variety of fruit and vegetables, including citrus trees, grapes and potatoes. They suck the sap out of plants and leave a honeydew residue behind that can quickly start to mold. Lacewings and mealybug destroyers enjoy eating mealybugs, so do what it takes to attract them to your garden. Companion planting isn't an effective means of eliminating mealybugs.

Mexican bean beetle

The Mexican bean beetle is a connoisseur of several varieties of beans. It has a bottomless pit for a stomach and will continue chewing on the leaves of a plant until it starts to die. These beetles roam the Western half of the United States, looking for bean crops to devastate.

The following plants are known to repel Mexican bean beetles:

- Garlic.
- Marigolds.
- Rosemary.

Japanese Beetles

Japanese beetles are commonly found in the Eastern half of the United States and are known to attack a variety of vegetables and flowers. They are a bluish-green color and feature rust-colored wing covers. They are pretty to look at, but the damage they can do to a crop is anything but pretty.

The following plants will deter Japanese beetles:

- Catnip.
- Chives.
- Chrysanthemums.
- Garlic.
- Marigolds.
- Onions.

Scales

Scales are aptly named because, immediately, they look like small scales attached to a plant. They are destructive little creatures that will suck sap from plants during every stage of their life cycle. When you notice scales on your plants, prune them back to get rid of the affected areas or scrub them off the branches.

There are no plants that are known to deter scales, so you'll have to rely on predatory insects to get the job done. Ladybugs, praying mantises and green lacewings will all dine on scales, so plants that attract them may help.

Thrips

These tiny insects are so small you probably won't see them on your plants. What you will see are discolored areas that take on an almost silvery sheen as the thrips bite into the plants repeatedly and leave a large number of tiny little scars. Thrips aren't problematic unless the population gets out of control and begins to spread viruses.

Tomato Fruitworms (Corn Earworms)

Tomato fruit worms, also known as corn earworms, cotton bollworms and geranium budworms, are found in gardens throughout North America. These worms are known by several names, usually indicative of the type of plant they're attacking. They've been known to dine on cotton, beans, peas, peppers, tomatoes, corn, geraniums, potatoes and squash.

The adults are small moths that lay eggs on the bottoms of leaves. The larvae feed on the leaves as they grow. If they're attacking a corn crop, they'll move into the husks as the corn matures and will eventually begin to feed on the silk and the corn kernels at the ends of the ears.

Geraniums and thyme are known to deter the tomato fruit worm.

Tomato Hornworm

This large caterpillar is found in gardens throughout the United States, usually munching on the leaves of eggplant, peppers, potatoes and tomatoes. They develop into large moths that have a wingspan of up to 5".

The following plants will repel tomato hornworms:

- Borage.
- Dill.
- Thyme.

CHAPTER 5: GARDEN PLANNING

The key to successful companion planting is properly planning where the plants in your garden are going to go. You've got to carefully consider how each of the plants in your garden is going to interact with one another and then place them in the best possible locations to take advantage of those interactions. The biggest limitation concerning companion planting is the knowledge of the gardener. Arm yourself with as much knowledge as possible before you ever put on your gardening gloves.

The first step to proper garden planning is deciding which plants you want in your garden. Create a master list of the plants you need to have and plan your garden around that list. Once you have a list of essential plants, supplement the list with a handful of other plants you wouldn't mind having.

Now, get to work researching the potential interactions between the plants you need and the plants you'd like to have. Consider allelopathy, pests, beneficial insects, the heights of the plants, and the depths of the root systems to create groupings of plants that will work hand-in-hand. Plants that are beneficial to one another should be kept together, while plants that are detrimental to each other should be planted at opposite ends of the garden.

Once you've got your garden planned, take a closer look at the plants you've included in the plans and see if there are any other plants you didn't include that can help. Flowers, ground cover and other smaller good neighbors may be able to be squeezed into small areas of the garden to good effect. With companion planting, you aren't going to have your typical garden with row after orderly row of produce. Instead, you're going to have plants that are mixed and matched because of what they can do for one another.

Don't start planting until you've got your garden mapped out. It's the best way to ensure you keep good neighbors together and bad neighbors far apart.

Alfalfa

Alfalfa is primarily grown as a forage crop because it's easy to grow and is a high-value feed crop that's high in protein. It prefers deep, well-drained soil, but can be grown in a wide variety of soil types. Alfalfa sprouts can be consumed by humans, but full-grown plants are generally used for animal *feed*.

As far as the home garden is concerned, alfalfa is generally planted as a cover crop that can be grown between crops that place a heavy load on the soil. Plant your garden with alfalfa and turn it into the soil and you'll ensure successive gardens have the nutrients they need to successfully grow.

If you've got hardpan or thick clay soil, alfalfa can be used to break up the soil. It has a deep rooting system and has even been known to push roots through rocks. Avoid planting alfalfa around tomatoes because it is allelopathic toward tomato seedlings.

Known Benefits: Alfalfa increases the level of iron, magnesium, nitrogen, phosphorous and potassium in the soil. It can also be planted to increase the amount of green foliage in the garden to confuse pests looking to land on something green. Additionally, alfalfa crops can be planted to provide habitat for predatory and parasitic insects that will prey on pests.

Almonds

If you live in a climate warm enough to grow almonds, consider yourself very lucky. It can take up to 5 years for young trees to start producing, but once they do you'll be able to harvest almonds from them annually for up to 50 years. A single healthy, full-grown tree can produce upwards of 40 pounds of almonds per year.

Almond trees are good to plant around blackberries because they hold moisture in their canopies and drop leaves that turn into mulch.

Known Benefits: Almonds can hold moisture in their leaves. When the leaves fall they turn into natural organic mulch.

Anise

Anise is a strong-scented herb that has the flavor of licorice. It grows tall, so it can be used to provide shade for low-growing plants. It's said to improve the vigor of any plant grown nearby and is a popular choice for flower beds.

Coriander especially benefits from being grown near anise because it speeds up germination. Broccoli and other Brassica family plants benefit from anise because it masks their smell, preventing pests that target their scents.

Known Benefits: Anise is known to deter lice and some biting insects while attracting predatory wasps that prey on aphids. The strong scent of anise masks the scent of nearby plants, hiding them from pests.

Apples

Apple trees are a great addition to most backyards. They run the gamut from huge trees that reach more than 25' in height to smaller dwarf or hedge varieties that only grow to 8' to 10' tall, so there's an apple tree for almost any yard. Apple trees can be grown in containers, so you may even be able to grow apples if all you have is a concrete patio.

Apricots

Many apricot varieties are early bloomers and may not be a good choice for areas that get late frosts because a good frost can kill the bloom. When choosing a variety, carefully consider whether you want an early-, midseason- or late-blooming tree.

Apricot trees can reach 30' in height and a single tree can produce up to 100 pounds of apricots. Apricot trees can live up to 70 years.

Asparagus

Asparagus is a dinner-time favorite that tastes equally great whether lightly oiled and tossed on the grill, boiled or steamed. Asparagus stalks can grow to heights of 5' or more but are rarely allowed to do so because they become woody and inedible. Harvest asparagus for eating when it's around 8" to 10" in height.

This hardy plant is good neighbors with several plants and gets along well with most neighbors. When paired with basil, it's believed to draw in ladybugs that keep aphids out of the garden. Comfrey is a good choice because it dies back as the asparagus starts to grow and will provide food for the growing asparagus plants. Just be aware that comfrey can grow out of control and may need to be cut back to give asparagus space.

Known Benefits: Asparagus can be planted around low-growing plants and will provide mottled shade for the plants during the heat of the day. Planting asparagus near tomato plants will help repel the nematodes that attack tomatoes.

Asters

This brightly-colored flower blooms well into the late summer and fall and can add color to a garden long after most summer blooms have lost their luster. Asters range from small in stature at 6" to 8" to very tall, with some varieties reaching heights approaching 8'.

While asters are compatible with most vegetables, they need to be kept away from celery and corn because they're carriers of aster yellows disease, which can cause deformities in the flowers of the aster plant. Asparagus thrives when planted near asters because they repel harmful nematodes and a handful of other insects.

Known Benefits: Attracts pollinating insects and ladybugs, while repelling nematodes and other insects.

Basil

Basil is a bushy annual garden herb that can grow up to 2' tall. It's a highly fragrant plant used in a wide variety of dishes as a seasoning herb.

Basil is beneficial when planted near most garden crops, as it aids with growth and repels many insects. When paired with asparagus, basil is thought to draw ladybugs into the garden. When planted closely to tomatoes, both plants end up tasting better.

Known Benefits: Basil helps deter fungal growth and is capable of driving away from several insects, including aphids, asparagus beetles, mites, and mosquitoes. In addition to driving away bad insects, basil also attracts butterflies, which can aid with pollination.

Bay

Bay leaves come from the bay laurel tree, which is an evergreen tree native to Greece. It prefers a moderate climate and doesn't do well in areas that experience deep freezes. Bay can be grown in containers, so that may be an option for those looking to grow bay in a cooler climate.

Known Benefits: Bay leaves will deter weevils and moths. This effect is more pronounced when bay leaves are dried and crushed and dispersed into the soil.

CHAPTER 6: COMPANION PLANTING CHART

SOWING, PLANTING DATES AND TEMPERATURE CHART

Remember that you will have to use this guide to fit in with the temperature and weather conditions in your local area. Even within one small area, there can be variations due to prevailing winds, hills, valleys, etc. Your seed packets will provide you with general guidelines buy you will need to consult an experienced local grower for more exact information.

The most important information they can give you will relate to local frost times. This is the key piece of information for using this chart. This is because the sowing dates and planting out dates are based on the approximate date of the last frost in your locality.

Peppers/Chili

Sow 8 weeks before the last frost date.	Germination occurs within 10-21 days
Germination temperature needed is 80-85°F	Plant out 2 weeks after the last frost date.

Tomatoes

Sow 6 W before the last frost date	Germination occurs in 7 – 10 days
Germination T needed is 75 - 80°F	Plant out 2 W after the last frost date.

Broccoli

Sow 8 W before the last frost date	Germination occurs in 7 – 10 days
Germination T needed is 70 - 75°F	Plant out 3 W before the last frost date.

Cabbage

Sow 8 W before the last frost date	Germination occurs in 6 – 9 days
Germination T needed is 70 - 75°F	Plant out 3 W before the last frost date.

Cauliflower

Sow 7 W before the last frost date	Germination occurs in 5 – 10 days
Germination T needed is 70 - 75°F	Plant out 3 W before the last frost date.

Kale

Sow 8 W before the last frost date	Germination occurs in 6 – 9 days
Germination T needed is 70 - 75°F	Plant out 3 W before the last frost date

Eggplant

Sow 8 W before the last frost date	Germination occurs in 10 – 14 days
Germination T needed is 80 - 90°F	Plant out 2 W after the last frost date.

Leek

Sow 10 W before the last frost date	Germination occurs in 5 – 10 days
Germination T needed is 75 - 85°F	Plant out 2 W before the last frost date.

Lettuce

Sow 8 W before the last frost date	Germination occurs in 3 – 5 days
Germination T needed is 65 - 75°F	Plant out 4 W before the last frost date

Onion

Sow 10 W before the last frost date	Germination occurs in 7 – 9 days
Germination T needed is 70 – 75°F	Plant out 2 W before the last frost date

Basil

Sow 3 W before the last frost date	Germination occurs in 5 -7 days
Germination T needed is 70 - 80°F	Plant out 2 W after the last frost date

Marjoram/Oregano

Sow 6 W before the last frost date	Germination occurs in 7 – 10 days
Germination T needed is 65 -75°F	Plant out 2 W after the last frost date.

Parsley

Sow 10 W before the last frost date	Germination occurs in 10 – 14 days
Germination T needed is 70°F	Plant out 2 W before the last frost date.

Canterbury Bells

Sow seeds 5 to 7 W before the last frost date. Germination T needed is 60 - 70°F	Germination occurs in 10 – 20 days. Plant out 2 W after the last frost date.

Carnations

Sow seeds 9 – 10 W before the last frost date. Germination T needed is 65 - 75°F	Germination occurs in 10 -20 days. Plant out 2 W before the last frost date

Columbines

Sow seeds 2 – 5 W before the last frost date. Germination T needed is 70 - 75°F	Germination occurs in 20 25 days. Plant out 6 W after the last frost date

Delphiniums

Sow 2 – 5 W before the last frost date	Germination occurs in 10 – 20 days
Germination T needed is 65 - 75°F	Plant out 4 – 7 W after the last frost date.

Foxglove

Sow seeds 10 – 12 W before the last frost date. Germination T needed is 65 -70°F

Germination occurs within 14 -21 days
Plant out 2 W before the last frost date.

Lobelia

Sow seeds 6 W before the last frost date
Germination T needed is 65 - 70°F

Germination occurs in 10 – 14 days
Plant out 2 W after the last frost date.

Marigolds

Sow seeds 6 – 7 W before the last frost date. Germination T needed is 75 - 80°F

Germination occurs in 5 – 7 days
Plant out 2 W after the last frost date.

Nicotiana

Sow seeds 6 -7 W before the last frost date. Germination T needed is 70 -75°F

Germination occurs in 14 – 21 days
Plant out 2 W after the last frost date

Viola/Pansy

Sow seeds 10 – 12 W before the last frost date. Germination T needed is 65 - 70°F

Germination occurs in 10 -14 days
Plant out 2 W before the last frost date

Petunia

Sow seeds 10 -12 W before the last frost date. Germination T needed is 75 -80°F

Germination occurs in 10 -14 days
Plant out 2 W after the last frost date.

Phlox

Sow seeds 4 W before the last frost date
Germination T needed is 60 - 65°F

Germination occurs in 9 – 15 days
Plant out 2 W after the last frost date.

Snapdragons

Sow seeds 10 – 12 W before the last frost date. Germination T needed is 65 – 70°F

Germination occurs in 7 - 14 days
Plant out 2 W before the last frost date.

Statice

Sow seeds 6 – 7 W before the last frost date. Germination T needed is 70 -75°F

Germination occurs in 7 – 14 days
Plant out 2 W after the last frost date.

1.1   QUICK REFERENCE COMPANION PLANTING CHART:

VEGGIES	GOOD COMPANION	BAD COMPANION
Asparagus	tomato, parsley, basil	onions, garlic, potatoes
Beans	beetroot, cabbage, celery, carrot, cucumber, corn, squash, pea's, potatoes, radish, strawberry.	garlic, shallot or onions
Beets	broccoli, brussels sprouts, bush beans, cabbage, cauliflower	charlock, field mustard, pole beans
Cabbage	cucumber, potato, onion, spinach, celery.	Strawberries
Carrots	beans, peas, onions, leeks, lettuce, tomato, and radish	Dill
Celery	bean, tomato and cabbage family	corn, Irish potato and aster flowers
Corn	potato, pumpkin, squash, tomato, cucumber	Tomatoes
Cucumber	cabbage, beans, radish, tomato	late potatoes
Eggplant	beans, peas, spinach, tarragon, thyme	

Garlic	cabbage, cane fruits, fruit trees, tomatoes	peas, beans
Leeks	Carrots, celery, onions	Legumes
Lettuce	carrot, beet, onion, and strawberry	cabbage family
Melon	pumpkin, radish, corn, and squash	
Onions	cabbage family, beet, tomato, pepper, strawberry, and chard	beans, peas
Parsley	asparagus, carrot, tomato and corn	Mint
Peas	beans, carrot, corn and radish	garlic leeks, onions, shallots
Peppers	tomato, eggplant, carrot and onion	fennel, kohlrabi
Potatoes	bean, cabbage, squash and peas	apples, cherries, cucumbers, pumpkins, sunflowers, tomatoes
Pumpkin	melon eggplant and corn	potato, raspberry
Radish	carrot, cucumber, bean, pea, melon	Hyssop
Squash	melon, pumpkin, beans, cucumber, onion	potato, tomato
Strawberry	bean, lettuce, onion and spinach	cabbage, broccoli, Brussels sprouts

Tomatoes	celery, cucumber, asparagus, parsley, pepper and carrot	fennel, kohlrabi, potatoes

1.2 BENEFICIAL HERBS

Many herbs can be extremely beneficial for your companion planting. Indeed the herbs themselves can lend that extra dimension to your vegetable garden, that will complement your vegetables – and improve your cooking!

Here is a list of some popular herbs along with the benefits they may have to certain plants.

Anise:

Anise is known to benefit beans and coriander plants.

Basil:

This is known to benefit asparagus, beans, cabbage and especially tomatoes.

It can be beneficial also as a 'sacrificial' plant in that it's soft leaves tend to attract butterflies and boring insects.

Caraway:

This is an ideal herb for breaking down and conditioning poor soils. It also attracts the attention of wasps and other harmful insects, making it a good 'sacrificial' herb. Also known to benefit strawberries and peas.

Chives:

An ideal companion for carrots, as it confuses the carrot fly. Also good around peppers, potato, rhubarb, squash or tomato plants, as it deters insects – particularly aphids.

Fennel:

This makes a poor companion plant for just about anything – avoid planting near other plants.

Lavender:

A good companion plant for many species as it's aromatic flowers attract many beneficial, pollinating insects to the garden.

It will also deter fleas, ticks and even mice!

Mint:

This is another all-round beneficial companion for many plant species; and in particular, peas, cabbage and tomatoes.

Mint is known also to deter insects, and even mice from your plants.

Parsley:

Asparagus is known to benefit particularly well, when grown alongside parsley; but carrots, cor, sweet peppers are also good companions.

Avoid planting near mint or lettuce.

Peppermint:

A good companion as it attracts beneficial insects and repels ants, aphids and cabbage fly.

CHAPTER 7: WAYS TO FEED YOUR GARDEN

There are many options available to feed your garden. Some require commercial fertilizers, but the best are ones that you can use without adding chemicals to the soil. These include:

- Monoculture
- Rotation
- Mulches
- Compost
- Garden teas
- Fertilizers

MONOCULTURE

Monoculture is the process of planting just one type of plant. In companion planting, this practice is used to enrich the soil through the benefits one plant can give. This monoculture plant is then turned back into the soil to increase the nutrient level of the soil. One example of this is to grow alfalfa or another grass crop and turn it back under before it goes to seed to let it decompose further before planting that area of your garden. By doing this, the soil has a chance to rest and replenish itself.

ROTATION

Crop rotation is a great way to control insects, weeds, and diseases, and it also enhances soil fertility. Vegetables in the same botanical family will require similar nutrients in similar amounts. Some will be considered heavy feeders like broccoli, sweet corn, and tomatoes, and will utilize more of the soil's nutrients, whereas others are considered light feeders, like carrots, onions, peppers, and potatoes, and will use fewer nutrients. To go along with these plant types, some plants add nutrients and improve the soil, like peas and beans. If you practice crop rotation by alternating these three types of crops in one bed, the soil can be enhanced.

MULCHES

Mulch is a protective layer placed over the soil. There are many benefits to using mulch including:

- Minimizes weeds — the mulch will suffocate weeds and stop light from reaching the seeds, which stops new weeds from germinating.
- Improves the garden plants — the mulch covers the plant's roots that are on the surface, saving them from damage caused by cultivation and drying out.
- Retains moisture — mulch reduces the amount of evaporation, which keeps the soil moist, and allows for more even growth.

• Minimizes temperature differences — the mulch minimizes the temperature extremes at the soil level so it stays warmer at night and cooler in the day.

• Improves the soil — if you are using organic mulch, it will add nutrients to the soil as it decomposes, encouraging microbial growth. It also encourages earthworms to burrow in the soil, which aerates and drains the soil. The mulch also prevents the soil from packing down.

• Creates a more even-looking garden — mulch stops the dirt from splashing up onto the plants during rain or watering and from washing the soil away from the plants during too heavy rain or watering.

• Gives the garden a finished look — the garden looks professional with a nice mulch covering it. A uniform layer of good-looking mulch throughout the garden gives the area a uniform, "finished" look.

The following are some forms of mulch you may want to consider.

Organic Mulch

There are many types of organic mulch to choose from. There are some you may have readily available and others you may need to buy. Most will be available through your local garden center.

The best organic mulches include:

• Bark or small wood chips — these come as small or large chips (or chip your own if you have a wood chipper) and work well under trees and shrubs. You can purchase finely shredded cedar mulch in various colors that can add an interesting designer component.

• Leaves — fall leaves are great for mulching large open areas, particularly around the squash, pumpkin patches, or other sprawling areas. If you are short on different type of mulch, like compost or newspaper, leaves make a great second layer. Not only does it cover up something unsightly, but it also helps with decomposition.

• Eucalyptus — this mulch has to be purchased from your local garden center and comes shredded or as fiber mulch. The advantage of this type of mulch is that the oil in the eucalyptus repels termites, fleas, ticks, and insects. The disadvantage is that it can be hard to obtain and it can be twice as expensive as other types of mulch.

• Grass clippings — when they are fresh, they are smelly and will stain your hands but are high in moisture and nitrogen, making them good for the garden. Avoid using clippings that are full of grass seeds because these seeds are likely to sprout in your garden. This mulch is easy to work with and can be placed throughout the garden where the seedlings are more delicate or closely planted, such as around lettuce, spinach, and carrots.

• Straw — if you have access to straw, it offers excellent winter protection for your garden. The only problem with using a straw is the potential for some of the seeds to germinate. Straw should be seed-free but because it is often confused with hay, which still has seeds, it is possible to end up with seeds in your bales. Another disadvantage is that it is not very attractive and looks worse as time goes on.

• Pine needles — this is a long-lasting mulch that can slightly acidify the soil under it. This makes it good for potatoes and strawberries, which benefit from the more acidic soil. It is also an easy mulch to put into small or hard-to-reach places. Pine cones can also be used and make an attractive addition to any woodland garden.

• Pine bark — this is a mulch that decomposes slower than other varieties and will last a year or more. It comes in different sizes, ranging from fine to 2-inch chunks. The disadvantage of this mulch is that it can lower the pH slightly. You can still use it around the same plants that prefer a more acidic environment like strawberries.

Non-Organic Mulch

There are several non-organic mulches available on the market. These types of mulches keep the weeds down and do not need replacing like organic mulches. Some of these mulches include:

• Plastic sheeting — these are large sheets of dark plastic. They are great to use in the spring to warm up beds and are also great for suppressing weeds. If you use a heavy grade plastic, which will last many years, you can lay it down between rows of plants where you want more heat, like between tomatoes, or on paths where you want to suppress weeds. You can use the sheeting to help improve the soil by stuffing the underside of the black plastic with organic matter to compost underneath the sheet. Some gardeners even lay the plastic down and cut holes into it to transplant seedlings. The plastic can stay on throughout the whole season as a weed suppressor. The problem with doing this is that it will not let water through it.

• Landscape fabric — this is a loosely woven fabric that helps retain moisture and slows or even prevents weed growth. The disadvantage of this type of mulch is that is usually one of two layers with a top layer covering the fabric to make the garden bed look better. Also, consider that some landscape cloths are nonporous and will not let moisture through. If you purchase the nonporous type, the plant roots can suffocate and rot.

• Rubber — this product is made from recycled tires and will not decompose, making it permanent mulch. It can be purchased as mats, tiles, and nuggets and is available in various colors. It will not blow away or wash away under heavy watering. It also comes in many attractive colors, giving it a strong design element. In practical terms, insects avoid the rubber and it does not sink into the ground like gravel and rocks. However, the product can give off a strong odor and can be both expensive and hard to find.

• Stone (pebbles and gravel) — stones can be as small as pea gravel or as large as small boulders. The small gravel will stop the weeds better, but when topped with an assortment of boulders, together they create a nice contrast for the garden. Stones are another permanent cover as they do not break down over time but offer great color and texture to a garden. The disadvantage is that some of the smaller rocks will disappear into the soil over time and working with this type of mulch is physically demanding.

WHEN TO MULCH

Lay the mulch down in the garden after the soil has warmed up in the late spring or the early summer. Placing an even, a shallow layer of mulch approximately 2 to 4 inches deep will be effective against wind, sun, weeds, and pests. Be careful of the plants and avoid putting the mulch close to the crown of the perennials and the stems or trunks of shrubs and trees as you do not want to damage new growth and you need to leave plants space to obtain water.

If you live in a winter climate, one of the best times to mulch is in winter.

Depending on where you live, the freezing and thawing process causes the soil to expand and contract. This can break new roots and even force your plants out of the ground in a process called frost heaves. If you cover the garden with something loose and full of air, like straw, when the ground first freezes, you can help keep the ground frozen until winter ends. Once spring arrives, you can remove the mulch.

Another benefit of winter mulching is protecting all types of plants, including perennials and ground covers, from winter burn, which can happen when the winter temperatures damage the plants. When the ground freezes and there is a strong wind, the moisture is pulled from the plant.

COMPOST

Compost can be the best natural fertilizer for your garden, regardless of the type of plants you are growing. It is a mixture of decomposed plant and animal material (manure) and many other organic materials that then go through decomposition in the presence of oxygen, called aerobic decomposition, to create rich black soil. This soil is excellent for your garden as a soil conditioner and fertilizer.

The best compost materials include fruit and vegetable material, garden trimmings (not weeds gone to seed), and animal manure from horses, goats, sheep, and chicken. Other materials to consider adding if you have them available include leaves, coffee grounds, paper, cardboard, seafood shells, tree bark, eggshells, and even "humanure" (human waste).

How to make compost

Choose a spot close enough to be easily accessible but out of sight. You can choose to purchase a compost bin or build a system to work in the space you have available. You can make a heap in one corner of the garden and use the area to make your compost pile; you can use a single bin and place all the organic material into it, or you can create a three-bin system (made from wood). If you leave the bins open on one side, you can easily add to the pile, and turn it over occasionally. Only cover the tops of the compost bins if your area receives a lot of rain. The three-bin system allows you to turn the compost from one bin to the other so that the compost in the final bin is ready to use while the pile in the second bin is in the middle stage and the first bin is just starting to decompose. However, you will need to manually move the compost from one bin to the other.

When starting a new compost pile, making a pile with two parts of brown materials to one part green will help the materials break down faster. The green garden materials are grass clipping or old annual plants pulled from the garden, and the brown garden materials are dry leaves and twigs. The green material is high in nitrogen and the brown material is high in carbon and both are required to make your compost work successfully. If you add in too much green, the compost will have a foul odor.

Pile or layer the green and browns into a heap until you have a compost heap that is about 3 feet by 3 feet by 3 feet. You want the pile close to this size because it will heat up quickly and will therefore break down faster. Once a week, check the moisture content of the pile. To decompose properly, your pile will need water, but if there is too much moisture, the pile will not be able to maintain the required heat level. Your compost should feel damp like a wrung-out sponge; any more water content than this and the pile will start to smell worse than normal. If your pile is too wet, you can add more leaves; if it is too dry, you can water it gently with a garden hose.

Once a week, the pile needs to be turned over, meaning you turn the outside material into the center – where there is internal compost heat. Oxygen is required for the decomposition process, which is why you turn the pile. Turning the pile also stops it from becoming hard and compacted. Some people keep a perforated PVC pipe standing upright in the center of the compost pile to let oxygen reach the center of the pile.

If you turn your pile over once a week, you could have finished compost in eight to ten weeks. The compost pile that is not turned over will not be as active and will take longer to decompose with the good compost sitting at the bottom of the pile. During the decomposition process, the temperature of the pile will reach between 110 and 160°F. You can monitor the temperature with a long probe thermometer pushed into the center of the pile. Turn the pile when the temperature drops below the 110°F mark to speed up the composting process. If you decide not to monitor the temperature, you can turn the pile every month.

The compost from the bin system is ready when the temperature lowers until it is barely warm and the original materials in the pile are no longer recognizable. You may have a few pieces that are not quite "finished," which is fine; throw them into the first bin to start the next pile of compost. The compost should also be a rich black-brown color, moist, and have an earthy smell.

How to use compost

Now that you have this great rich soil, it is time to add it to your garden. If you do not want any bits left in your compost, you can run it through a compost sifter, which is wire mesh in a frame, that will leave you with only soil. The bits and pieces that do not go through the sifter can go back into the compost pile. You can do several things with this nutrient rich-soil but treat it as you would any rich fertilizer or potting soil. There are several ways you can use your compost:

• As a mulch to hold water — you can spread it about 3 inches thick on the base of plants, trees, shrubs, or perennials in the garden. If there are some unfinished pieces in your compost, they are fine to use here as they will continue to break down over time.

• To fertilize the garden — you would want to dig the compost into the existing garden, going down several inches or more to work the compost in.

• To make a compost tea — some compost tea is a natural byproduct of compost. If there is no liquid in your compost, you can steep a shovel full of compost in a bucket of water for a few days. After a few days have passed, remove the compost material, put it back in the compost pile, and simply water the plants with the compost tea. If you want, you can put the compost into something like an old towel, cheesecloth, or burlap bag before putting it into the bucket of water.

- As a topping for your lawn — often called a lawn dressing, you can add a 1- to 3-inch layer of compost on top of the existing grass. The compost works its way into the ground as the grass grows through it. Because it is a great way to fertilize the grass, adding compost in the spring or fall may eliminate the need to fertilize throughout the rest of the season.

Many people add the compost into their gardens in fall or spring, whenever it is ready, digging it in as they turn their beds over. Whichever way you choose, your plants will benefit from adding compost.

CHAPTER 8: PERFECT COMBINATIONS

Some plants really work best with each other, which is why they are considered "perfect combinations". Here are some of that you may want to try yourself.

• Cabbage and Tomatoes. Tomatoes can repel the Diamondback Moth larvae which are infamous for chewing cabbage leaves and leaving large holes in them.

• Nasturtiums and Cucumbers. Cucumbers make use of Nasturtiums as trellises while Nasturtiums can repel the dreaded cucumber beetles. They also serve as a natural habitat for ground beetles and spiders which are predatory insects.

• Ragweed/Pigweed and Peppers. Ragweed and Pigweed are good weeds that can make the soil fertile and can protect plants from being infested by pests.

• Corn and Beans. This combination has been used for thousands of years, as you've read at the beginning of this book, and they are both able to attract beneficial insects such as leaf beetles and leaf horns. Aside from that, they also provide shade and trellis to each other, making sure that they both grow well and become beneficial for humans.

• Dill and Cabbage. They support each other in the sense that dill attracts wasps that eat pests and worms, making sure that the cabbages grow without holes.

• Chives and Roses. Garlic repels the pests that feed on roses, and they also look great when they are planted next to each other.

• Tall Flowers and Lettuce. Tall flowers such as Cleomes and Nicotiana give lettuce shade.

• Sweet Alyssum and Potatoes. Tiny flowers of sweet alyssum attract predatory wasps and also act as a shade for the potatoes.

- Catnip and Collard. They reduce beetle damage.

- Spinach and Radishes. They are both able to repel leaf miners and radishes can grow safe and well when planted with spinach.

- Dwarf Zinnias and Cauliflower. Dwarf Zinnias are great because their nectar lures predatory insects like ladybugs, and they are known to hunt down and eat common garden pests.

- Melons and Marigold. Marigold repels nematodes just as well as chemical treatments do.

- Love-in-a-mist and Strawberries. They are great for aesthetic purposes.

Here are a couple more companion plants that you can plant in your garden:

- Anise. Anise is a good host for predatory wasps which repels aphids and also camouflages the odor of the other plants to protect them from pests. Anise is best planted with Coriander or Cilantro.

- Amaranth. Amaranth is an annual plant that grows mostly in tropical conditions and is very beneficial when planted near sweet corn stalks. It acts as a shade for the corn which can moisten the soil and allow corn to grow better and faster. Amaranth also plays host to ground beetles which are predatory insects who feed on common pests.

- Bay Leaf. Bay leaf repels moths and weevils and can also act as a natural insecticide. Bay leaf is best planted with Tansy, Cayenne Pepper, and Peppermint.

- Beets. Beets add minerals to the soil, especially nitrogen that most plants need to grow. They are great fertilizers for the soil, too, as they contain 25% magnesium and are best planted with melon and corn.

- Bee Balm. When planted with tomatoes, bee balm can improve the growth and flavor of the tomatoes. Bee Balm also attracts bees and butterflies for pollination and is also great for aesthetic purposes as it always looks good and fresh.

- Buckwheat. Buckwheat is a good cover crop as it is full of calcium and is also able to attract beneficial insects such as butterflies and bees, and repels pests such as aphids, flower bugs, pirate bugs, and predatory wasps away. Buckwheat can also provide the soil with phosphorous which other plants may also be able to benefit from.

- Chards. Chards are good not only as vegetables but also as ornamental plants that make pollination possible by attracting beneficial insects. They are best planted with tomatoes, roses, beans, onions, and cabbages.

- German Chamomile. This is an annual plant that can improve the flavor of cucumbers, cabbages, and onions and also act as a host to wasps and hoverflies. German Chamomile also gives the soil protection by providing it with sulfur, potassium, and calcium and also by increasing oil production in the herbs. Because of increased oil production, more people can benefit from their plants by making different kinds of aromatherapy oils.

• Clover. Clover works as a cover crop or green manure and is best planted near grapevines to attract beneficial insects and make pollination possible. When planted around apple trees, they can repel wooly aphids and also reduce cabbage aphids once planted near cabbages. Clover is also able to increase the number of ground beetles that are great for destroying non-beneficial insects.

• Castor Bean. Castor bean is a poisonous plant that is very effective in repelling moles and mice. And because it is poisonous, you need to be careful where you plant it.

• Chrysanthemums. Fondly called "mums", they can repel nematodes which destroy most plants easily. They are also used as botanical pesticides as they are full of Vitamin C that repels most pests, especially Japanese beetles. They work well with daisies in attracting beneficial insects in pollinating your garden.

• Comfrey. An underrated plant, Comfrey is beneficial because it gives calcium and potassium to the soil and also is a good medicinal plant. It also prevents foliage and is a good compost activator as well as a nutrient miner. It is best planted with avocadoes.

• Costmary. This flowering plant is very effective in the repulsion and killing of moths.

• Dahlia. While it looks harmless, the dahlia is able to repel nematodes.

• Four-o-clocks. These flowers can poison the dreaded Japanese beetles but you also have to be careful because being around these flowers too much is also toxic to humans.

• Flax. Flax is used in most diets and is full of linseed oil and tannin that are very useful against the Colorado Potato Bug.

• Hemp. Hemp is very useful when planted near brassicas as it can repel bugs and pests.

• Hyssop. Hyssop can repel cabbage moths and flea beetles and is best planted with grapes and cabbages. Hyssop is also able to attract bees which is good for pollination. More often than not, bees make hyssops their homes, which is good for you as this means that your garden will be pollinated even more.

• Horehound. Horehound belongs to the Mint family and can attract beneficial insects such as Icheumonid and Braconoid wasps that consume flies and other insects that feed on your plants.

• Lamium. Many gardeners and farmers think that Lamium is awesome because it can repel potato bugs which infest most plants and are not good for anyone's garden.

- Lavender. Lavender provides you with great essential oils and is also able to repel non-beneficial insects such as moths and fleas. It is also able to protect plants from whiteflies. Lavender is best planted during the winter season so it could bloom in spring.

- Larkspur. Larkspur can kill Japanese beetles but you have to be careful around it as it is also poisonous to humans.

- Marjoram. Marjoram can improve the flavor of most fruits and vegetables and also attracts butterflies and bees so pollination could happen. It's always best to grow sweet marjoram as it gives the best results.

- Morning Glory. Morning Glory attracts hoverflies and also makes the garden more beautiful as it is a vine.

- Stinging Nettles. These plants attract bees and are also full of calcium and silica that are essential for invigorating plants and improving resistance to diseases and also give the soil the nutrients it needs for plants to grow healthy and well.

- Okra. While it is not a vegetable favored by many, Okra is very useful as it gives shade to lettuce especially during the summer season, and prevents the lettuce from wilting. It is also able to protect eggplants and peppers from strong winds. It is also great when planted with peas, cucumber, basil, and melons as it also repels aphids away.

- Opal Basil. Opal Basil grows annually and can repel hornworms. It is best planted with oregano, petunia, asparagus, and peppers and must be kept away from sage and rue.

- Peach. Peach Trees give shade to asparagus, grapes, onions, and garlic and may help repel tree borers and most other pests and insects.

- Hot Peppers. Hot peppers protect most plants' roots from being rotten and provide shelter for smaller plants, especially chili peppers and prevent other plants from being dried up or wilted. It is best planted with okra, green peppers, and tomatoes.

- Pennyroyal. A great plant that repels fleas, mosquitoes, gnats, flies, and ticks.

- Purslane. Is a good cover crop for corn and makes the soil healthy and fertile.

- Rye. Prevents germs from targeting your plants and is great when planted near tomatoes and broccoli as well as with other vegetables.

- Soybeans. Soybeans provide nitrogen for the soil and also repel Japanese beetles and chinch bugs.

- Turnip. Turnip is also able to provide a lot of nitrogen to the soil and is best planted with peas and cabbage. Do not plant near potatoes though as turnip stunts their growth.

- White Geraniums. White Geraniums are effective in repelling Japanese beetles.

CHAPTER 9: HOW TO GET STARTED

Once you know which plants you want to grow and what your primary goals for companion planting are, it's time to get your system into action.

COST, MATERIALS, LOCATION, AND TIME

The cost of establishing a new garden can be quite variable, depending on many factors. First among them is whether you want to start your garden from seed or buy seedlings that are already somewhat established. Seeds are far less expensive than seedlings, but the advantage of the latter is that you can plant them right away in a prepared bed, instead of starting them indoors and transplanting them.

Assess your budget and how much time you want to commit to getting the garden started and base your decision on that. To maintain a companion garden, you don't need too many materials. A source of water is of course essential, whether it is a rain barrel, well pump, or spout. Beyond that, a sturdy spade, a garden rake or hoe, and a trowel are all you need to garden with. These are the gardener's basic toolset, and with them you can maintain any patch of the garden easily. While you can buy them new, if you are on a budget you can always look for them at garage sales or thrift shops. Make sure you are getting good quality, however – they will get a lot of use, and you don't want flimsy tools that will wear out easily. Locate your garden in an area that gets a lot of sun through the growing season. You can assess the sunlight simply by checking shadows throughout the day to see which areas get the most light. Very simply, you do not want tall buildings or trees shading the area you will locate your garden in. Additionally, the garden should be in a well-drained area.

Do not locate your garden at the bottom of an elevated area that will flood it with rain runoff. And if you can locate it conveniently close to your house, it will make maintenance and harvest a much easier job. The amount of time you spend on your garden is also based on several factors, such as the size of the garden, how many different plants you are growing, and how eager you are to invest a lot of effort in maintaining it.

But the majority of your time will be spent on establishing the garden: one of the major benefits of companion planting is that it saves you a lot of time on a day-to-day basis.

Since the plants are providing one another with nutrients, pest control, and weed control, you don't have to spend as much time performing these tasks yourself.

Be prepared to spend a few afternoons establishing your garden, and after you've done so, you won't have to spend more than an hour or two a week on watering, checking for pests and weeds, and monitoring the plants' growth and vitality.

COMPOST AND SOIL MAINTENANCE

For starters, you will need to prepare productive, healthy soil. Whether you are adopting a new or unused piece of ground to a companion garden space, it can be tempting to try to finish the preparation phase as quickly as possible and get straight into production. But building soil with the right texture, with a good blend of different sized mineral particles and organic matter, will help ensure your plants have the best foundation to grow well.

Your companion garden will need rich, healthy soil to be fertile and productive. The amount of time you spend preparing the soil will pay off huge dividends in the long run, so it is certainly worth it. Your crops' vigor and overall health will be greatly affected by how effectively you prepare the soil. The most productive garden soil has 5-10% organic matter: this includes fallen bits of plant and animal detritus, decaying leaves, and humus. While this amount does not seem particularly large, just a small amount of organic matter can go a long way to ensuring the soil is healthy. Decaying organic matter provides nutrients to the soil and improves its structure, creating a loose, crumbly loam that is easier for roots to move through. It helps small particles of clay bind together into larger pieces, which improves drainage, and it helps to hold water in the soil that would normally be dry, sandy, and infertile.

To build up the organic content of your garden bed, add about an inch of compost or well-finished livestock manure every year as an amendment to the soil. You can also add coarse mulch such as four inches of straw or dead leaves. If you have deep, raised beds, you will need to add more organic matter, and the same applies if you are working in a particularly hot climate, in areas that are heavily used, or if you have sandy or heavy soil.

It's also important to make sure the soil is properly aerated. This ensures that microscopic life can flourish, creating the right conditions for organic matter in the soil to be broken down into nutrients the plants can use. In a smaller garden, you can use a spade or spading fork to turn the soil. Loosen the top eight to twelve inches as much as you can, and work compost or manure into it as you do so. Use a hoe or a rake to break up clumps of soil and form a smooth, level surface.

If the soil in your garden is particularly heavy or rich with clay, you may want to consider renting a rotary tiller to break it up. These machines have churning tines that cut through dense soil. While they do not dig as deeply as you can with a spade, the depth they provide will usually be enough, particularly if you plan to establish raised beds. While renting a rotary tiller costs more than turning the soil by hand, you can usually finish the job more quickly with one. If your garden plot is particularly large, it can be well worth the investment.

CREATING GARDENS IN LIMITED SPACES

In a companion garden, you can organize planting arrangements in many different ways, based on your goals and the amount of space you have. One of the major advantages of companion planting is that it allows you to get more out of smaller spaces because you can mix crops in ways that maximize the amount of space available.

Double Rows are a simple way to combine two types of crops. This is a great technique for growing bush beans or cucumbers alongside lettuce or other greens. This system allows you to grow a weed-suppressing canopy (or "natural mulch") that reduces the amount of work you have to do. Double rows are also a great way to plant climbing vegetables on either side of a trellis.

Wide Rows can be up to five feet across. This is just wide enough that you can reach the plants in the middle of the row from either side. This allows you to walk around the bed instead of on it, which will help prevent soil compaction. The broad growing area lets you plant several kinds of companion plants in a staggered formation or side by side across the row.

Wide rows are perfect for growing lots of small plants like leafy greens and root crops in a small area. You can interplant leaf lettuce, carrots, radishes, and onions in staggered rows in the spring. You can also grow larger plants in a wide row, with insect-repellant flowers around the outside.

LOCAL CLIMATE CONDITIONS AND WHAT TO GROW

Climate conditions can be astonishingly variable from one latitude to the next, and because of that, you must find out what hardiness zone you live in. Hardiness zones are geographically defined climate regions that have similar growing conditions throughout. They've generally arrayed along fairly well-defined latitudes, but can be subject to the effects of geographical features such as mountains, large bodies of water, and local climate conditions.

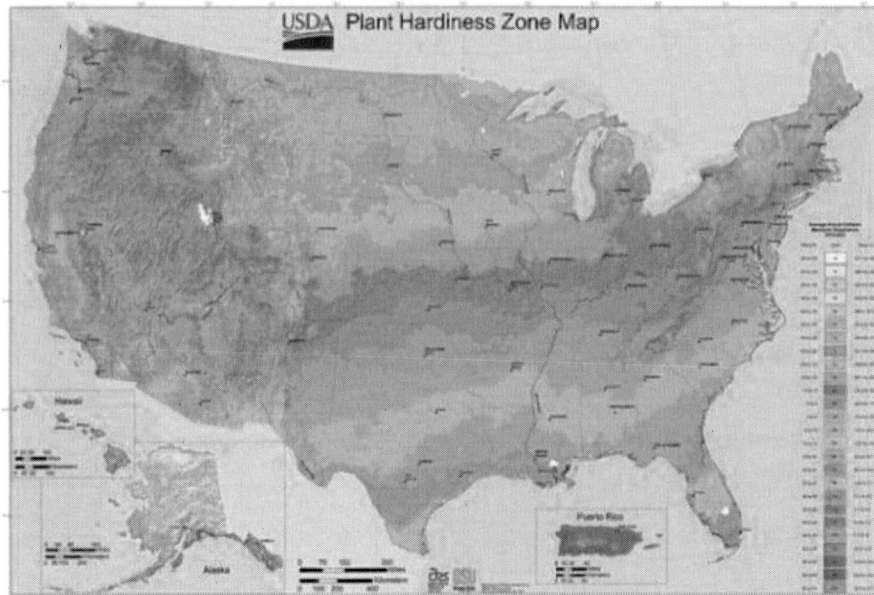

USDA Plant Hardiness Zone Map

All regions of the world have hardiness zone maps available that will tell you what is best to grow there as well as when local frost dates generally occur. Familiarize yourself with these frost dates as well as what plants are best suited to grow in your region's hardiness zone.

Different Methods

There are a few different companion planting methods that have been shown to work particularly well. You may have already heard of some of them. The three sisters' technique, square foot gardening, container gardening, and the seven-layer system known as the forest garden are some of the most popular.

The Three Sisters

This is a companion planting technique that was developed by Native Americans to enhance the growth conditions of some of their staple crops: corn, beans, and squash. This technique uses the companion methods of structural support and nutrient cycling. Three or four bean plants are planted around the base of each corn plant in rows, with squash planted between the rows. The beans fix nitrogen in the soil for the corn plants, which in turn provide structural support for the bean vines. The squash also benefits from the nutrient cycling of the beans, and its broad leaves provide natural mulch to shade out weed plants.

Square Foot Gardening

Square Foot Gardening is a companion technique designed to increase the amount of yield from a small garden space. In this method, long rows are abandoned in favor of a grid system. The grid is composed of 1' x 1' squares, and each square is dedicated to a different crop. This method allows the gardener to intercrop numerous cultivars in the same location more easily. This is useful because, with a square foot garden, you can incorporate companion plants, pest repelling flowers, attractive plants to lure pollinators and predatory insects, and cycle nutrients. This allows you to get the most effective companion planting system in the smallest space.

Container Gardening

This is a useful method for making the most of small spaces, as well as gardening when you only have a balcony, rooftop, or patio available to work with. You can apply any of the principles of companion planting to your container garden for pest control, nutrient cycling, and structural support just as you would if you were planting in the ground. An additional aspect of companion planting in containers is the fact that you have more spatial variability to work with. You can trail creeping vines from the edges of containers, especially if they are hanging baskets. And you can build successively taller layers in the container, working from the outside edge inwards.

1. CANOPY (LARGE FRUIT & NUT TREES)
2. LOW TREE LAYER (DWARF FRUIT TREES)
3. SHRUB LAYER (CURRANTS & BERRIES)
4. HERBACEOUS (COMFREYS, BEETS, HERBS)
5. RHIZOSPHERE (ROOT VEGETABLES)
6. SOIL SURFACE (GROUND COVER, EG, STRAWBERRY, ETC)
7. VERTICAL LAYER (CLIMBERS, VINES)

THE FOREST GARDEN: A SEVEN LEVEL BENEFICIAL GUILD

The Seven Layer System

This is an intensive companion planting method in which the garden is structurally modeled after the composition of a forest. Forests have complex understories with multiple ecological levels. In a seven-layer garden, tall fruit trees make up the upper canopy layer. The next layer is composed of smaller nut trees or dwarf fruit trees. Below this is a shrub layer with berry bushes, followed by a layer of medium-sized vegetables. The lower layers include root and tuber vegetables and a ground cover of edible plants that propagate horizontally. The final layer is made up of climbing vines that grow up through the other layers.

1.3   COMPANION PLANTING FOR PEST CONTROL

Of all the benefits that companion planting can provide your garden, controlling pests is probably one of the most important ones. While companion planting can't eradicate garden pests, it can help reduce the damage caused by them significantly. Effectively companion planting to control pests starts with observing your garden, doing some simple research, and planning.

Begin by looking for obvious signs of pests in your garden. Are certain plants doing poorly? Are there visible pests or signs of disease? If there are holes in the leaves, you could be dealing with beetles, slugs, or caterpillars. If there are tunnels in the stems, borers are the most likely culprit. If plants are wilting or growing poorly, there are probably aphids, thrips, or leaf hoppers present. Check under the leaves and along the stems, since this is where many pests like to hide and lay their eggs.

Once you know what kind of pests you are dealing with, you should learn everything you can about it. Find out about its life cycle, when it typically appears in the garden, and whether it attacks just certain plants or a wide range of them. Once you have this information, you will be ready to start combining plants to protect against the attackers.

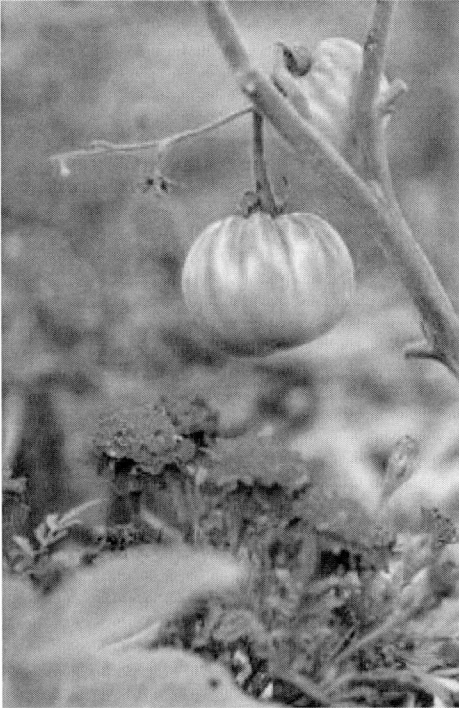

Tomatoes and Marigolds

HOW PLANTS DETER PESTS

Plants discourage pests with several different strategies. Some kinds of plants only use one method; others use a combination of properties to fight pests. You can use all of the following methods in your garden to make pests unwelcome.

Making detection difficult is a great way to throw pests off the trail of your vegetables. Many pests are attracted by the smell of certain plants. The cucumber beetle, for example, is attracted to cucumbers by cucurbitacin, a bitter compound. Other pests find their targets using visual cues like color.

Because of this, you can fool pests by planting off color cultivars of their favorite vegetable. Red cabbage, purple cauliflower, and purple kohlrabi are less attractive to cabbage loopers. Yellow berries attract fewer birds than red berries do. Japanese beetles are less attracted to dark-colored flowers. Some plants are less attractive to pests because of their structure or location. Aphids prefer the shade, so they'll pass by exposed pea vines in favor of densely branched plants.

Repelling attacks is the next line of defense. Once pests find a target plant, they have to break through its natural defenses, such as tough, hairy, or waxy leaves that make penetration harder. Hairy-leaved tomatoes, for example, deter many chewing insects. Other kinds of physical defenses can help reduce pest damage. Corn ears with long, tight husks are less prone to damage by earworms or birds. Beans and peas that have tough, leathery pods can resist injury by weevils.

COMPANIONS AS REPELLENTS

Take advantage of the natural ways plants can repel pests in your companion garden. You can mask the scent of certain crops with more pungent species, use plants and their extracts to deter or kill pests, and create physical barriers to keep flying, predatory insects from flying away from your garden.

Powerfully scented plants produce various chemical compounds that can discourage most pests. Bold citrus or perfumed fragrances are given off by the volatile essential oils in the mint, thyme, lemon balm, and lemon geranium often drive pests away. Many herbs produce these compounds, making them natural choices as companion plants.

Mixing these strong-smelling plants among crops that are prone to pest attacks can help mask the scent of target vegetables and keep them safe. Garlic is another very strong-smelling plant with a well-deserved reputation as an excellent companion plant. It is often recommended for interplanting with roses or tomatoes to keep pests away. Garlic also has fungicidal and bactericidal properties that can protect tomatoes from blight.

DECOY AND TRAP CROPS

Growing plants that you know pests will be attracted to might sound crazy, but it's a great way to use companion plants to your advantage. The trick is to plant a few cultivars that pests will find more attractive than your good crops. The pests will be more likely to damage the decoy plants than your crops. Trap cropping does take some advance planning and careful observation.

Your trap crops must already be growing when insects are out in force. If the pest problem only occurs at a single time of year, a single planting of trap crops can be enough to control them. But if a pest tends to be active through the growing season, you will need to plant a succession of trap crops. For example, you can sow nasturtiums among your tomatoes and roses every two weeks throughout the summer.

As soon as you find aphids swarming on one crop of nasturtiums, destroy the plants and the pests quickly so the aphids don't have a chance to reproduce. Keep trap crops like nasturtiums as close as you can to the target crops. Watch them carefully and be ready to kill the pests before they breed or move on to other targets.

CHAPTER 10: COMPANION VEGETABLES

This offers you an in-depth look at how to plant various vegetables and the best and worst companion plants to go with them. Remember that most vegetables like nutrient-rich soil full of well-rotted compost and mulches. Even if the individual plant instructions do not mention this fact, make sure your garden bed is richly prepared before beginning. There are a few vegetables that do well in sandy beds, like carrots, but most do better in well dug over dirt that has been enriched with nutrients in preparation for the long growing season. All beds will also benefit from additional nutrients throughout the growing season.

The following are guidelines you can follow, but take the time to make this fun. Mix up the planting and interplant carrots with beets and radishes or try planting kohlrabi with both to take advantage of the nutrients at the surface level versus deeper root levels. Vegetable gardening can be a fun and rewarding experience.

ASPARAGUS

Asparagus prefers to grow in the same spot year after year, so pick a full-sun location for best results or partial shade in a spot where it will not need to be disturbed. You will need to purchase asparagus crowns from your local garden center or nursery catalog. The crown will have a strong root system but the top growth will be dormant. Plant the crowns in early spring for most locations; if you live in a warmer climate, you can plant in late winter. The asparagus will need to be planted deep so make a trench approximately 6 to 7 inches deep. Spread the bottom of the trench with wood ashes or bone meal and compost if you have it. There will be instructions on the asparagus when you purchase it, so make sure you read and follow them.

In general, soaking the roots first, preferably in compost tea, is a good start. Then lay them on their side in the trench approximately 1 foot apart. Make sure the rows are 3 to 4 feet apart. You will fill in the trench slowly as the sprouts appear but only cover the stalks and be sure to leave the foliage uncovered. With time, the trench will fill in and the asparagus foliage will now be above ground level. It is important to be diligent with the weeding and you should aim to lay down mulch once the trench is filled in.

Asparagus has many companion plants, including the family of aster flowers, dill, coriander, basil, comfrey, and marigolds, which will deter beetles. Parsley appears to increase the growth of both plants when they are grown together. Tomatoes and asparagus help each other; tomatoes protect against asparagus beetles and a chemical in the asparagus juice deters nematodes from tomato plants. There are no known bad companions for asparagus; however, these plants do better when they are not close to onion, garlic, or potatoes.

Beans

There are different types of beans available, like snap, dry, and bush. Some will have different companions, both good and bad. Some basics apply to all types of beans. Plant in a full-sun location or partial shade if you live in hot climates. Sow seeds only after the danger of frost have passed. For scarlet runner beans, which are climbers, supply support of some kind. Thin the seedlings to 5 or 6 inches apart but leave slightly more space for pole beans.

All beans can enrich the soil with nitrogen. They all do well when planted with carrots, cauliflower, peas, radishes, potatoes, strawberries, the brassica family, chard, and corn, and they are of great benefit to cucumbers and cabbage. Summer savory is another good companion to beans as it improves the beans' growth and flavor and deters the bean beetles. Marigolds, rosemary, and nasturtiums also deter bean beetles.

Bad companions for beans include garlic, onion, and shallots as they appear to stunt the plants' growth. They are not happy planted close to gladiolas. Beans are prone to diseases, but crop rotation will prevent most of them. There are also companions specific to individual types of beans.

BUSH BEANS

Bush beans, a shrub variety of the snap bean, do well with celery if planted at the ratio of one celery plant to six bush beans. Bush beans do well close to celery and leeks but only if there are only one or two bean plants there. If more than this is planted, then none of them do well. Bush beans will give and receive benefits when planted with strawberries and cucumbers. Bush beans are a bad companion to fennel and onions.

POLE BEANS

Pole beans, a climbing variety of bean like scarlet runner beans, do particularly well with corn, summer savory, and radish. They do not particularly like beets. They make bad companions with onions, beets, cabbage, eggplant, kohlrabi, and sunflowers.

BROAD BEANS

Broad beans also called fava beans or horse beans, produce large, flat pods with large beans inside. They are excellent companions for corn, potato, cucumbers, strawberry, celery, and summer savory. They are bad companions with onions.

BEETS

Beets are an easy-to-grow crop that prefers a full-sun location and well-tilled soil with good drainage. They germinate well and will need to be thinned to 4 inches apart with rows at least 2 feet apart. Beets are great for the garden as they add minerals to the soil.

Beets are good companions for lettuce, onions, kohlrabi, and the brassica family. Mint, garlic (which improves the beet's flavor), and catnip help beets grow. If you do not want to plant mints around the beets, you can use mint foliage as mulch. Beets are bad companions to pole beans and give mixed results next to bush beans.

BROCCOLI

Broccoli grows best in full sun or partial shade in well-drained soil. In terms of minimizing disease, plant broccoli where no other brassicas (including cabbage, Brussels sprouts, kohlrabi, and cauliflower) have been planted in the last two years as per crop rotation rules. Broccoli is a large plant and can reach 3 feet in height so the seeds or nursery seedlings should be planted 18 inches apart after the danger of frost has passed. If they do not form heads (broccoli florets) properly, they are deficient in lime, phosphorus, or potash. You can purchase these nutrients at your garden center and add them to your broccoli plants.

Broccoli, like all the brassicas, does well with aromatic plants including dill, which improves the plant's growth and health. Broccoli is a good companion to beets, celery, chard, cucumber, lettuce, onion, potato, and spinach. Flea beetles like broccoli so plant Chinese Daikon and Snow Belle radishes to attract flea beetles away from the broccoli.

Do not plant close to tomatoes, strawberries, pole beans, peppers, or mustards as they are bad companions.

CABBAGE

Cabbage needs to spend at least half the time in the shade. You can grow from seed or purchase the plant from a nursery to get a jump on the season. Insects like young cabbages so consider covering the plants with a light-weight cloth when they are first growing. They love compost, fertilizer, and water. If the cabbage's florets do not form properly, the plant is deficient in lime, phosphorus, or potash and you should purchase some from your local garden supply store to add to your beds.

Cabbage, like all the brassica family, does well with aromatic plants including dill, while sage, peppermint, and rosemary help repel cabbage flies. Celery and dill improve cabbage's health and growth. Clover will reduce native cabbage aphids and cabbage worms. Other good companions include onions, potatoes, hyssop, thyme, and southernwood. Wormwood repels white cabbage butterfly. Tansy deters cabbage worm and cutworm, and thyme deters cabbage worm. Nasturtium deters bugs, beetles, and aphids from cabbage.

Bad companions for cabbage are strawberries, tomatoes, peppers, lettuce, eggplants, rue, grapes, and pole beans.

CARROTS

Carrots prefer full sun and need a very loose, preferably sandy soil for the roots to grow easily downward. If your soil is high in lime, humus, and potash, you will have sweeter tasting carrots. Low nitrogen levels in the soil will decrease the flavor of your carrots. Sow seeds directly into the garden several weeks ahead of the last frost (in warm climates you can sow in fall, winter, and spring). Sow seeds around ½ inch deep and thin to 3 to 4 inches apart. Thin early before the roots entwine and be careful to not damage the remaining plants.

Plant onions, leeks, rosemary, and sage to deter the carrot fly. Other good companions include lettuce, onions, chives, beans (which are a good source of nitrogen and can help increase your carrots' flavor), peas, peppers, radish, and tomatoes. Tomatoes can stunt the carrot's growth but they will have a great flavor. Bad companions for the carrot are dill and parsnip. If you want to use carrots to attract insects, they need to be able to flower, so plant a few carrots to leave them in the ground instead of harvest them for eating.

CAULIFLOWER

Cauliflower likes a full-sun location in well-drained soil. Purchase nursery stock to get a jump on the season or sow outdoors after the danger of frost has passed. Sow in small clusters of several seeds but once they have sprouted, keep only the strongest cauliflower plants. Keep the plants moist when they are young.

For growing instructions and companions, see cabbage as most members of the brassica family have similar growing requirements.

CELERY

Celery needs to have a lot of sunshine but can have partial sun for half of the day. Celery requires rich, moist soil. It is easiest to work with plants from the nursery that you can transplant into the garden when there is no danger of frost. Plant 8 to 10 inches apart and be generous with compost and water over the growing season.

Good companion plants for celery include beans, leeks, onions, spinach, tomato, and the brassica family. Garlic and chives help keep aphids away from celery. If bush beans and celery grow together, they will strengthen each other. Friends of celery include cosmos, daisies, and snapdragons. Bad companions for celery are corn, lettuce, and aster flowers.

CHARD

Chard is an easy-to-grow vegetable. It prefers full sunlight unless you live in a hot climate where they prefer partial shade. Well-drained soil with compost helps chard produce well. For most climates, sow the seeds in the spring and thin to 8 inches apart when the seedlings are about 6 inches high. You can either eat these seedlings or transport them to another spot in the garden.

Good companions for chard include beans, brassica family members, and onions. There are no known bad companions.

CORN

Corn likes full sun and a rich, well-draining soil covered in the mulch. Sow several seeds in a hill approximately 1 inch deep and 6 inches apart. When seedlings are close to 4 inches tall, thin them to 1 foot apart. Corn needs a steady supply of water and mulch.

Corn helps beans when grown together (as in the Three Sisters example) and sunflowers, legumes, peanuts, squash, cucumbers, melons, amaranth, white geranium, lamb's quarters, morning glory, parsley, and potatoes all help corn. Marigolds help to deter the Japanese beetle away from corn. Planting radishes around corn and letting them go to seed deters an insect called a corn borer, which is known to be a pest for several agricultural crops. Bad companions for corn are tomato and celery. Pigweed is said to raise nutrients from the deeper earth level to a place where the corn can reach them.

CUCUMBER

Cucumbers like full sun and can also do well with afternoon shade. Seeds are sown several inches deep a couple of weeks after the danger of frost has passed and once the soil has warmed slightly. Plant the bush varieties approximately 1½ feet apart and the vine varieties 2 to 3 feet apart.

Cucumbers have many good companions including corn, beans, sunflowers, peas, beets, and carrots. Radishes can deter cucumber beetles. Keeping dill close to cucumbers attracts beneficial predators and cucumbers attract ground beetles. Nasturtiums improve the cucumbers' growth and flavor. Bad companions for cucumbers include tomatoes and sage.

EGGPLANT

Eggplant loves heat, so plant it where it can have full sun. It is easiest to purchase started plants then transplant them when there is no longer any danger of frost. It is preferable to wait a week or two after frost has passed to allow the soil to warm up. There are dwarf and standard varieties of eggplant. Plant the standard versions approximately 1½ to 2 feet apart and the dwarf varieties can be 1 to 1½ feet apart. Tie the taller varieties to stakes to keep the fruit from touching the ground.

Good companions for the eggplant include amaranth, peas, spinach, and marigolds, which deter nematodes. Eggplant helps beans and peppers. They are good to plant with corn as they deter raccoons from eating the corn and the corn protects the eggplant from a virus that causes wilt. Bad companions for eggplants are pole beans, fennel, and potatoes. There are mixed results when planted with aromatic herbs.

HORSERADISH

This is an easy plant to grow and will take over your garden in no time. Find a corner away from most of the plants and consider planting horseradish in containers. It is easiest to purchase a small plant from the nursery and it will grow in most conditions. Plant 1 foot apart and bury the top of the root 4 inches below the surface. Make sure you water this plant well.

If you grow this plant in a container, you can move the containers around. Keep 1 plant in the potato patch to deter the blister beetle and help deter the Colorado potato beetle. Horseradish also improves the potatoes' resistance to disease. If you are going to plant it in the potato patch, be sure to dig it up and remove it in the fall to prevent the plant from spreading.

KOHLRABI

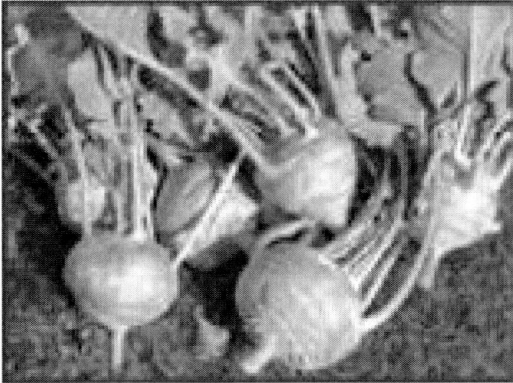

Kohlrabi is a cooler weather vegetable that can be planted for both spring and fall crops. Plant in full sun and well-drained soil. Sow seeds outside four weeks before the last frost. Plant the seeds ½ inch deep and 3 inches apart but thin them to 6 inches when the seedlings are several inches high, which will not take very long as these plants are very fast growing.

Kohlrabi is a good companion with cucumbers, beets, onions, and chives and appears to help protect members of the mustard family. It is a bad companion to strawberries, tomatoes, peppers, and pole beans.

LEEKS

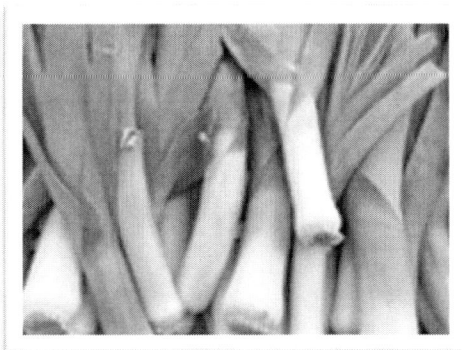

Leeks like a full-sun location that offers well-drained soil. It is easiest to buy leek plants to transplant into the garden around the time of the last frost. Place the seedlings approximately 6 inches apart. Set the plants closer together if you are planting long, thin-stemmed varieties or set them wider apart for thick-stemmed varieties. (Always check the package for specific planting instructions.) Make a hole and set the seedling down so that only an inch of the top of the plant is exposed. Fill it in loosely with soil.

Leeks will improve the growth of celery, onions, and apple trees. Carrots help leeks by repelling carrot flies. Bad companions for leeks are legumes including beans and peas.

LETTUCE

Lettuce does best with a mixture of sun and shade. It does not like the extreme heat and will need shade during the hottest months or else it will go to seed. Sow the seeds outdoors once the ground has thoroughly thawed and can be worked. If you purchased plants, set them approximately 1 foot apart (this may vary based on the variety so read the label) and sow several times for a lettuce supply all summer.

Lettuce does well when close to radish, onions, kohlrabi, beans (both bush and pole), cucumbers, carrots, strawberries, beets, and sunflowers. Chives and garlic are great deterrents of aphids so plant them close to lettuce. Mints like hyssop and sage repel slugs so plant these plants close to your lettuce if slugs are a problem in your area. Lettuce is a bad companion to celery, cabbage, and parsley.

ONIONS

Onions are another plant where it helps to purchase plants at a nursery instead of starting the plant from seeds. You can transplant onions into your garden up to two months before the last frost is expected. Any earlier than this and it could be too cold for them. They like a partial to sunny spot and appreciate compost. Make sure the soil is dug over well to allow for good bulb development and weed constantly in the early growth stage as the weeds can crowd out the young onion plants. As the bulbs grow, make sure to keep them covered if they start to push out of the ground.

Good companions for the onion include all the brassicas, beets, lettuce, tomatoes, summer savory, leeks, kohlrabi, dill, lettuce, and tomatoes. Plant onions in the strawberry patch to help the strawberries stay healthy and fight off disease. Pigweed can raise the nutrients from subsoil and makes them available to the onions. Bad companions for onions are peas, beans, and parsley.

CHAPTER 11: BEGINNER MISTAKES TO AVOID

Just like heating up your interest in other things, you could also be burning with excitement over companion gardening. However, it is not always fruitful to be overly thrilled about something as you might oversee important details or perhaps rush things when you have to let time take its toll. This is true for companion gardening as well. Heating up the pot definitely helps but will not be able to sustain it unless you try to control the temperature.

STARTING TOO BIG

One of the most common mistakes that you should never attempt to do is to start big with companion gardening. Even if you have a big lawn or backyard intended for this purpose, you should always try a smaller plot first.

Consider your first plot as an experimental plot. When you have a smaller plot, you can manage it well and also observe if the plants that you have paired work. After all, since you intend to produce crops for personal use, then it could be best to have plots that you can readily manage rather than have several plots that you can't carefully attend to. It's a bad picture if you have plants dying in front of you.

NOT PREPARING YOUR SOIL

No matter how good the pair of plants that you intend to put into your garden, your labor will never bear much fruit if you have poor soil. Soil is the key to growing good produce, as plants typically are dependent on it for most of the nutrients necessary for plant growth, development, and propagation. Before starting your companion garden, you should prepare the soil.

First, the removal of weeds, rocks, and other unwanted debris is important as it may interfere with the optimal growth of your plants. Weeds may compete, not only for space but also for available minerals in the soil that may hinder or retard your crop's growth. It is also helpful if you study the profile of the soil in your garden so you can estimate also how much water will be necessary.

Clayish soils are gummy-like in appearance and when you hold them, the lumps are very visible. Such soil does not promote good air and water circulation and is not healthy for companion gardening.

Sandy soils, characterized by too many grains and breaking easily, also are not advisable for companion gardening as it allows water to drain easily. This may leave your plants wilting as water provided to them may not be absorbed readily by the roots as the grains of the sand are too fine to hold water molecules in place. Apart from draining water easily, sandy soils often have low nutrient concentration and are also unlikely to promote healthy crops.

Regardless of whether the soil in your garden is clayish or sandy, you can improve it by mixing compost into it. Decayed organic matter typically makes up the compost added to soils. It is a good source of nutrients for plants and at the same time improves the quality and texture of the soil. You can readily produce your compost by allowing leaves, peels, and other biodegradable items to degrade.

Composting is done simply by creating a layer of biodegradable items then covering it with soil. This is performed alternatively, then the compost pit is watered regularly to hasten degradation. Compost may also alter the pH of the soil and so it is important that you also measure this factor. Most plants grow optimally in neutral soil (pH 7) and others like camellias and rhododendrons prefer a soil of acidic pH. Lilacs and clematis also favor a more basic soil., keeping this in mind helps to augment your success in companion gardening.

ESTABLISHING PLOTS IN SHADY AREAS

Another thing to avoid in companion gardening is to position your garden in the shady section of the lawn or the backyard. Though other gardeners think of their convenience first when establishing their home plots, this is very beneficial in terms of achieving your goal of producing good quality crops or flowers. This is because sunlight is an important ingredient in a plant's physiological functions. The food-producing mechanism of plants can only be possible when sunlight is present. Though the requirements of plants for sunlight appear to vary, over-shading has never been known to help in crop production. Choose a site that is relatively exposed to the sun at the peak of the day.

EXCESSIVE WATERING

It's good to water your plants once established in the plots, but it is never fruitful to have garden plants watered excessively. Too much water may soak the roots and endanger them (as it may promote root rot) or it may actually destroy sensitive parts like buds and new leaves promoting early abscission. Fungal diseases like lights and powdery mildew are also associated with overwatering.

It is best to study the water requirements of the plants that you plant in your companion garden. For reference as to whether there's a need to water your garden or not, you can stick your finger on the soil (up to the second knuckle) and if the soil is dry, you may water the plants. However, if it is still wet, there is no need to add water to the soil. You should also avoid watering the plants from above.

If possible water it below the stem so that it ensures faster root absorption of available water and prevents wastage. Control the pressure when you water your garden. Too much pressure may not only break off some parts of the plants but will also promote soil erosion and root exposure.

COMPANION PLANTING CHART

PLANT	PARTNERS
Tomatoes	BASIL ASPARAGUS BROCCOLI GARLIC CARROTS CELERY ONIONS
Beans	CORN SQUASH RADISH BEETS SPINACH CUCUMBER POTATO
Peppers	BASIL ONION GARLIC SPINACH TOMATOES
Carrots	CHIVES ONION LEEKS TOMATO ROSEMARY CORIANDER LETTUCE RADISH
Lettuce	MINT CHIVES DILL BEANS BEETS ONION BROCCOLI
Potatoes	CORN CABBAGES PEAS SQUASH BEANS
Onions	CARROTS PARSNIPS LETTUCE CABBAGE BEETS TOMATOES ROSEMARY
Cucumber	CORN CABBAGE BEANS RADISH CELERY LETTUCE
Squash	CORN PEAS RADISH DILL BEANS
Corn	BEANS CUCUMBERS PUMPKINS MELONS
Peas	CAULIFLOWER GARLIC TURNSNIP RADISH POTATO CUCUMBER CORN BEANS

CONCLUSION

Thank you for making it to the end of **Companion Planting**, with this book as a guide, you can enjoy the benefits of companion planting to make your garden healthier and more productive, and without having to work as hard to repel pests or keep your crops robust. Starting with a solid foundation of healthy soil that is rich in organic matter, carefully plan out how to arrange your companion garden to get the most out of your space.

Companion planting is receiving a lot of attention from the scientific community because it can help reduce the need for harmful chemicals in farming. Home gardeners are re-discovering this information and using it to their benefit.

Remember that increasing yield is not just about spatial efficiency, but also about extending the growing season to be as long as possible. By applying the principles of companion planting, you can have a beautiful, productive garden that takes care of itself. Companion planting is an important way to shift to using more sustainable, organic methods of keeping your garden healthy.

Manufactured by Amazon.ca
Acheson, AB